TELECOURSE STUDY GU

MW01681032

PERSONAL FINANCE

FOURTH EDITION

ROBERT S. ROSEFSKY

Prepared by
SOUTHERN CALIFORNIA CONSORTIUM

contributing writers:
Herbert B. Long
Stephen Cyrus
Judy Sullivan

JOHN WILEY & SONS
NEW YORK CHICHESTER BRISBANE TORONTO SINGAPORE

Copyright © 1989, by John Wiley & Sons, Inc.

All rights reserved. Published simultaneously in Canada.

Reproduction or translation of any part of this work beyond that permitted by Sections 107 and 108 of the 1976 United States Copyright Act without the permission of the copyright owner is unlawful. Requests for permission or further information should be addressed to the Permissions Department, John Wiley & Sons.

INTRODUCTION

This is your study guide. Treasure it; struggle with it; use it as your personal road map to the world of PERSONAL FINANCE. Following the instructions in this guide will enable you to devote your time to absorbing course content rather than puzzling over what it is you are supposed to be learning.

Whether you are a newcomer to television courses or an old hand, it is important that you become familiar with the components of PERSONAL FINANCE, how they function with each other, and how they relate to you. Each of the elements in a telecourse contributes to the whole, effectively using the style of communication peculiar to that particular medium.

The Television Lesson

The video component of PERSONAL FINANCE calls your attention to key concepts and abstract ideas through a variety of formats. Using television for learning is not like watching a comedy series or sporting event. At first, you will have to concentrate on *active* watching. It is very easy to slip into the passive, half-viewing stance used for entertainment television. In most instances, you will have a chance to review the lesson in an alternate time period or watch videocassettes of the lesson at the learning center on campus.

If you have an audio recorder available, tape the audio portion of the program as you are viewing it. After you have watched the program and can visualize it, the audio portion is an excellent source for review. If you have any questions about content or wish additional information, contact the faculty adviser at the campus where you are enrolled.

The Text

The basic text for the course is *Personal Finance,* fourth edition, by Robert Rosefsky, published by John Wiley & Sons in 1989. The text is an essential part of the course, providing information most successfully adapted to the print media. It establishes a foundation of knowledge and elaborates on concepts introduced in the television segment through charts, case studies, and research. The assignment section of the study guide coordinates reading and review assignments from the text with the television segment.

The Study Guide

As the title indicates, the study guide helps you to synthesize and integrate the materials presented in the text and television segments. Each lesson of the study guide contains the following segments:

- □ **Overview-**A summary of the highlights of that particular lesson—major facts, concepts, and opinions placed in the total perspective of the course.
- □ **Learning Objectives-**The goals you are expected to accomplish as a result of completing the required activities for that particular lesson.

- **Key Terms and Phrases-**A vocabulary list of important words and expressions that will be encountered in the lesson. This segment complements, but is not a substitute for, the Glossary in the textbook.
- **Reading Assignment-**Required reading in the text that correlates with the lesson.
- **Self-Test-**A series of true-false and multiple-choice questions designed to test your understanding of the objectives of each lesson as well as to prepare you for the course examinations.
- **Using What You've Learned-**Opportunities to apply and practice what you have learned from the text and television lessons. You will be given the chance to plot your solution and test your knowledge without help. Any questions, discoveries, or difficulties may be shared with your campus instructor.

As we indicated earlier, each component in a telecourse contributes to the whole. The course is not any one of the elements by itself. It is a blending of all three: the television lesson, the text, and the study guide.

How to Use This Study Guide

These few suggestions may assist you in using this study guide and in understanding the rationale for its design.

First, read the Overview and study the Learning Objectives and Key Terms and Phrases for each lesson *before* you watch the corresponding television program. Each 30-minute television episode will go by too quickly for you to take comprehensive notes. Moreover, if you try to take notes on everything, you will soon discover that you have missed a great deal of the program. By completing all the pre-viewing requirements before watching the program, you are preparing yourself to select and retain those major concepts and facts not fully covered in the text. You will already have acquired the specialized vocabulary needed to understand the content of the television program, thereby eliminating one more obstacle in the learning process, and you will gain the ability to distinguish between what is truly important and what is interesting but incidental.

Second, it is a good idea to reread the assigned passages in the text as soon as possible after viewing the television lesson to reinforce what you have just seen.

Third, take the Self-Test honestly. Make a genuine attempt to answer each question without glancing first at the Answer Key. The Self-Test is your opportunity to practice what you have just learned, without penalty, and with almost instantaneous feedback. Make the most of this opportunity. Remember, the Self-Tests are a dry run for the examinations to come. Whenever you miss a question on the Self-Test, take the time to find out why. Use your errors to find out what fact or concept you missed or misunderstood along the way. You can learn as much from a wrong answer as from a right one and can avoid making the same mistake again.

Fourth, the activities in Using What You've Learned are designed to further your understanding of the objectives of each lesson, so they should be taken seriously.

Fifth, if you experience difficulty, seek help from the campus instructor. All of us who were involved in designing and producing this course hope not only that you will learn a great deal about personal finance but also that the whole process of learning will be an exciting and enjoyable one.

CONTENTS

PART ONE

BASIC CONCERNS

CHAPTER

1

The Economy

Overview

If there's anything to learn from recent history, it's that your financial affairs do not operate in a vacuum. Every day there are factors—some subtle, some direct—that can make your life better or worse. Some of these forces cannot be avoided, but many of them can be countered if you understand them and know what actions can be taken to avoid or neutralize their effects. This lesson will address those forces and influences that can have profound effect on your personal life and financial well-being.

The economy is similar to a make-believe football game. There are forces at work, and factors that influence those forces. And there are various results that occur depending on which forces have been influenced in what way. The effects, or results, can have a bearing on how you live your life. Further, the same forces and influences affect the economy of your city, state, and nation.

The basic forces in any economic entity are work power and human nature. **Work power** is the basic capacity of the population to work and produce. **Human nature** is more difficult to define. Much as a football team desires to win, any given population—be it a company, a family, or a government—has certain basic needs and desires. These include the desire to survive, the will to win, and the instinct to protect or expand territory. In the economic sense, aspects of human power can be expressed as expectations, greed, desire for power, and concern for the welfare of the citizens that make up the population.

There are far more influences in an economic entity than there are forces. Some of the main forces are listed below, briefly and in no particular order.

- **Information.** Education is to an economic population what training is to a football team. After the initial summer workouts, the quality of continuing education—practice and game experience—will further shape the team's success. In the economy, continuing education consists of an ongoing awareness of facts and trends. This information is available through a close scrutiny of the news media and specialized publications pertaining to one's pursuits.
- **Government policies.** Government policies and philosophies have a tremendous bearing on the forces at work in an economic population. Governmental influences include how the government taxes the people, spends money, and relates to other governments.
- **Management and labor.** Within a given company or industry, the quality of management is like the quality of coaching on a football team. The degree to which the workers cooperate with management is comparable to the team spirit or lack of it on the football team. This can also be viewed as a factor that affects productivity.
- **Technology or research and development.** The influence of technology cannot be overlooked, whether you are an individual examining job opportunities or the manager of a company exploring new and better ways to make products.
- **Nature.** A frozen or muddy football field can render the most powerful team ineffective. By the same token, a drought, flood, or an excessively cold winter can cripple the financial well-being of an otherwise healthy family, industry, or region.

- **Natural resources.** A family may have a naturally gifted musician, artist, football player, or entertainer, who can enrich the whole family's lives, both personally and financially. Likewise, a company may have a file drawer full of potentially profitable patents, or a nation may have untapped reserves of petroleum or minerals. Having natural resources is one thing; putting them to productive and profitable use is another.
- **Marketing.** Some people are better salespersons than others. The skills with which a product or service is packaged, advertised, and sold will have a strong bearing on the economic strength of a given entity.
- **Capital investment.** If an economic entity seems attractive enough to outsiders, they might be willing to invest in that entity. Such investments, put to proper use, can further enhance the well-being of the entity. An entity that is unattractive to outsiders can suffer accordingly.
- **The law of supply and demand.** This is a basic law of economics that can exert a powerful influence on attempts to succeed economically. If you grow watermelons and the harvest is bountiful, you may bring more melons to the market than people are willing to buy. It may be necessary to drop your price just to get rid of them and to avoid taking home unsold watermelons. And, even though you lower the price, you can still end up losing money. If the harvest is just right but the weather is cold when you come to the market with your watermelons, you can also lose. People may not want to venture out in the cold or may not develop the thirst that makes watermelons so attractive. In the first case, supply is greater than demand. In the second case, supply is just right, but demand is low. On the other hand, if your harvest is just right and demand is high, you could reap a tremendous profit on your watermelons.
- **Luck.** This is, to be sure, a very unscientific aspect of the science of economics. But it plays a role in almost all economic forces and influences. Whether it's a major or minor factor, good or bad, it's as unpredictable as it is unavoidable. The ability to take advantage of good luck and avoid the ravages of bad luck can make a distinct difference between success and failure in an economic endeavor.

As noted, these influences are not discussed in any particular order. In many cases, they overlap, intertwine, and influence each other. But whether taken individually, in combination, or in aggregate, significant changes in the economy occur when these influences and factors work together, including:

- inflation or deflation (rising or falling prices and wages)
- employment or unemployment
- growth of the economy, or recession
- survival of an economic entity or its termination
- an attractive investment climate or an unfavorable one
- surpluses or deficits

It is not the intent of this lesson to give you textbook definitions of such things as inflation, recession, deficits, surpluses, and other economic phenomena. Rather, it is hoped that the television segment and the text chapter will help you understand the influences at work in the world, our nation, and your own individual environment.

Learning Objectives

When you complete this lesson, you should be able to:

- List and describe the influences that shape and direct the economy.
- Explain the law of supply and demand and give an example of how it can affect your financial life.

- □ Define and give an example of inflation.
- □ State the purpose of a governmental monetary policy.
- □ Define productivity and state its importance to a country's economy.
- □ Cite recent examples of how the availability of natural resources have affected the American economy and of how technological advances have affected the American home and work life.

Reading Assignment

Read Chapter 1 of the text, "The Economy: How it Works and What it Means to You," pages 4–29.

Key Terms and Phrases

- □ **Deficit**—The status of a budget (one's financial condition) when more money has been spent than has been taken in, the difference being considered as debt.
- □ **Fiscal Policy**—The policy that determines how a government will raise money, and for what purpose it will spend it.
- □ **Monetary policy**—That part of a government's program that regulates the amount of money flowing through the economy.
- □ **Productivity**—A measurement of efficiency.
- □ **Surplus**—The status of a budget (one's financial condition) in which more money has been taken in than has been spent. (See deficit.)

Self-Test

1. The skills with which a product or service is packaged, advertised, and sold is known as technological research and development.
   a. true
   b. false
2. The law of supply and demand dictates that when a product becomes scarce, its price drops.
   a. true
   b. false
3. The part of a government's program that regulates the amount of money flowing through an economy is known as government monetary policy.
   a. true
   b. false
4. A company's ability to attract new investors of capital can mean greater career opportunities for its workers.
   a. true
   b. false
5. The economy of the United States entered a recovery period in 1982, characterized by reduced government spending, tax cuts, and a lower federal deficit.
   a. true
   b. false
6. Which of the following is an influence that gives shape and direction to the basic forces in an economic entity?

a. desire for power
b. national resources
c. marketing
d. all of the above

7. The policy whereby a government decides how to raise money for its support and decides how to spend that money is called
a. fiscal policy.
b. law of supply and demand policy.
c. management policy.
d. monetary policy.

8. If a government's monetary policy allows too much money in circulation, the economy is described as being in a period of
a. deflation.
b. inflation.
c. recession.
d. surplus.

9. Which of the following terms refers to the amount of work that can be generated by a given individual, considering the cost of the raw materials?
a. management
b. marketing
c. productivity
d. technology

10. The condition that occurs when more money has been taken in than has been spent is known as
a. inflation.
b. recession.
c. a surplus.
d. a deficit.

Using What You've Learned

Title: Your Career: Coping with the Future

Purpose: This project is intended to develop your awareness of the various influences that help shape and give direction to career development. It will help you develop a plan of action to cope with these influences.

Description: This project will require you to complete the following table by providing information that might have a bearing on your career development and advancement. Information can be obtained by reading, interviews, past history, and just plain common sense. The project enables you to examine in detail your chosen career and plan for your future.

Task: Complete the following table with information that applies specifically to your career. (See sample.)

Career Factors	Question and Information	Plan of Action to Cope with This Factor
1. Information and education needs	Career: Certified Public Accountant	
(SAMPLE)	1. What education is required to enter your career?	1. Obtain BS degree from XYZ University with major in accounting and minor in business administration, with at least B average. Enroll in MBA program at ABC University and concentrate on accounting courses.
	4-year college degree from an accredited college with a major in accounting. MBA degree is preferable.	
	2. What continuing education is needed?	2. Attend various workshops and seminars sponsored by state professional accounting agency.
	a. advanced graduate courses as needed	Read all new tax information provided by federal and state agencies.
	b. seminars and workshops that relate up-to-date information	Read professional journals.
	c. keep abreast of all federal and state tax laws	Read financial newspapers such as the *Wall Street Journal.*
	d. keep abreast of developments in the economy, domestic and international	Read weekly magazines such as *Business Week, Time, Newsweek.*

Career Factor	Question and Information	Plan of Action to Cope with This Factor
1. Information and education needs	Career: ________________ What education is required to enter your career? What continuing education is needed?	
2. Government policies	What federal, state, or local regulations and policies can affect your career? Are there any special law or license requirements?	

Career Factor	Question and Information	Plan of Action to Cope with This Factor
3. Management and labor	What are the past and current relations between management and labor? Are unions involved? Can you better advance in your career with or without union involvement?	
4. Technology	Is your career subject to technological changes and to what extent?	

Career Factor	Question and Information	Plan of Action to Cope with This Factor
5. Nature	Will a flood, drought, excessively cold winter, affect your career?	
6. Natural resources	Is a specific natural resource necessary to your career? Is it currently available? What about its future availability?	
7. Marketing	What is the past and current marketing strategy of your career product or service? To what extent does your career depend on the successful marketability of the product or service with which you are involved?	

Career Factor	Question and Information	Plan of Action to Cope with This Factor
8. Capital investment	Does your career depend on your company's or your own success in attracting new capital for its continued advancement? To what extent is this probable?	
9. Law of supply and demand	To what extent can you be affected by the law of supply and demand?	
10. Luck	What instances might occur in your career that would enable you to take advantage of being in the right place at the right time?	

Career Factor	Question and Information	Plan of Action to Cope with This Factor
11. Other	What other factors or influences can you foresee as having a bearing on your career?	

CHAPTER 2

Work, Income, and Your Career

Overview

The single most powerful force in shaping an individual's financial well-being is income-producing work. If you are to make the most of your occupation or career, it is necessary to look at work in a broader perspective than just something that fills the hours from 9 to 5. You must not look only at what you might be doing today, tomorrow, or next week, but where your aspirations and abilities can lead you. You must examine the many ways in which you can improve yourself and maximize the rewards and pleasures available through work. Finally, you must consider how you can most efficiently use the fruits of your labor—your income—to satisfy current and future needs and desires.

Factors in Choosing Your Work

Achieving your full potential is often interpreted as "success," and success is generally taken to mean making a lot of money. But there are important criteria other than money to be considered in choosing a field of endeavor; rewards such as self-satisfaction, the pride and pleasure of being creative and innovative, of being part of a winning team. Work can encourage personal growth and development and enhance your social, family, and community life. These rewards are often referred to as **psychic income.** You can't spend them, but they can be valuable. Your own ability to achieve the right sense of balance between monetary and psychic income will depend on a number of other factors, including:

- **Attitudes and aspirations.** Your choice of work, and your pursuit of sucess will be shaped not only by your own attitudes and aspirations but also by those of others around you.
- **Education.** It is generally acknowledged that education is the major foundation on which a successful career is built. The more education a person receives, the greater that person's potential for generating income is likely to be.
- **Aptitudes.** In a career sense, aptitude indicates that which you are best suited to do. But it doesn't necessarily indicate that enjoyment, fulfillment, or an acceptable level of income will be generated by exploiting that ability.
- **Personal experience.** Your own personal experiences, both at work and in private life, can affect your career choice and the success you achieve in a chosen career. Any prior work experience you may have had, whether paid or volunteer, can indicate whether you like a particular kind of work, whether you are good at it, and whether the general field interests you.

Seeking a job that leds to a career is a matter of selling. If a prospective employer is to buy your services on terms you are seeking, he or she must be convinced that your services will assist the company in generating a profit once you acquire the necessary training. In the selling process that we call seeking employment, advance preparation is most critical. Briefly, you will need to develop the following sales tools: a resume, references, and the ability to present your skills and yourself in an interview situation.

Beyond the base earnings you may be offered, it's essential that you carefully evaluate the full range of fringe benefits available in connection with your employment. Benefit packages can include pension plans, profit-sharing plans, health insurance plans, life insurance, educational programs, paid vacations, holidays and sick leave, and investment programs.

Your financial and legal rights as an employee are regulated and protected by a variety of federal and state laws. It's important that you be aware of how these laws can affect your work and income. The *Personal Finance* text summarizes the most important laws on pages 45–51.

Success, achievements, and advancements in your work and career will depend on more than just fulfilling your basic duties as an employee. Your awareness and active participation in achieving your employer's goals can enhance your value to the organization. Initiative, creativity, and willingness to cooperate can help move you up the ladder toward higher pay, greater recognition, and career advancement.

Learning Objectives

When you complete this lesson, you should be able to:

- □ Discuss the relationship between a college education and lifetime earnings.
- □ Define aptitude and analyze its role in career selection; define experience and its role in securing the job position you seek.
- □ List and evaluate the various fringe benefit options commonly offered by employers.
- □ Compare the major benefits available to the worker under Workers' Compensation, unemployment insurance, and Employee Retirement Income Security Legislation.
- □ State how each of the following pieces of legislation protects the worker against discrimination: the Federal Fair Labor Standards Act, the Age Discrimination in Employment Act, and the Fair Employment Practices Law.
- □ Indicate the relationship between the garnishing of a person's wages and his or her credit rating.

Reading Assignment

Read Chapter 2 of the text, "Work and Income," pages 30–55.

Key Terms and Phrases

- □ **Age Discrimination in Employment Act**—A federal law that protects workers between the ages of 40 and 65 with respect to hiring and firing problems because of their age.
- □ **Civil Rights Act**—See Fair Employment Practices Act.
- □ **Employee Retirement Income Securities Act (ERISA)**—A federal law that protects the rights of employees with respect to pension and profit-sharing plans; also known as the Pension Reform Law of 1974.
- □ **Fair Employment Practices Law**—A federal law designed to prevent job discrimination because of an individual's race, sex, religion, or national origin; also known as the Civil Rights Act of 1964.

- □ **Federal Fair Labor Standards Act**—A federal law that protects certain minors with respect to jobs that could be hazardous or detrimental to their well-being.
- □ **Federal Occupational Safety and Health Act (OSHA)**—A federal law that sets health and safety standards for working environments.
- □ **Garnishment**—A legal procedure by which a creditor can get access to a debtor's wages to satisfy a debt due the creditor.
- □ **Labor–Management Relations Act (1947)**—See National Labor Relations Act (1935).
- □ **National Labor Relations Act (1935)**—A federal law that regulates relations between employers and labor unions.
- □ **Pension plan**—A fringe benefit offered by many employers, whereby the employer puts aside a sum of money for the benefit of the employee upon retirement. Some plans also allow voluntary contributions by employees.
- □ **Profit-sharing plan.**—A fringe benefit whereby eligible employees receive a share of the company's profit, either annually or, more usually, on retirement.
- □ **Stock investment program**—A fringe benefit in which employees are offered the opportunity to buy shares of stock in the company at a lower price than they could on the open market.
- □ **Unemployment insurance**—A state-administered insurance program, paid for by employers, which provides financial benefits to employees who are laid off.
- □ **Workers' Compensation**—A state-administered health and disability program, paid for by employers, which provides certain benefits to workers who suffer job-related injuries or illnesses.

Self-Test

1. Work can be considered the single most powerful force in shaping your life-style.
a. true
b. false

2. You can control the amount of federal income tax withheld from your pay by varying the number of allowances you claim on your W-4 form.
a. true
b. false

3. If the money withheld from your paycheck for federal income taxes is greater than the amount you owe, the government will refund the overpayment with interest.
a. true
b. false

4. Even if you leave a job voluntarily, you are generally eligible for unemployment insurance benefits.
a. true
b. false

5. Under the Federal Wage and Hour laws, all workers are guaranteed a minimum hourly rate of pay.
a. true
b. false

6. An employer who is ordered to garnish your wages to satisfy creditor demands may discharge you because you have embarrassed the company.

a. true
b. false

7. Which of the following statements is most accurate?
   a. Male workers are less productive than female workers.
   b. Male workers are more productive than female workers.
   c. The percentage of males participating in the work force is increasing while the percentage of females is decreasing.
   d. Males are leaving the work force sooner because of earlier retirement programs.
8. Which of the following terms describes the number of years you must work for an employer before retirement benefits are set aside for your use upon retirement?
   a. garnishment
   b. profit sharing
   c. stock investing
   d. vesting plan
9. One of the primary purposes of the W-2 form is to
   a. allow your employer to withhold federal income taxes from your pay.
   b. enable the Internal Revenue Service to verify your total pay and the amount of federal income tax that was withheld from your pay.
   c. provide you with an opportunity to declare dependents.
   d. authorize the government to withhold federal income taxes from your pay.
10. Which of the following best applies to an Individual Retirement Account?
   a. An IRA can be a tax-sheltered benefit.
   b. An IRA applies only to self-employed individuals.
   c. IRA programs will gradually replace the Social Security program.
   d. The IRA is not a good investment because of the low interest rates.
11. Under the Fair Employment Practices Law,
   a. employers cannot refuse to hire you because of your race, color, religion, sex, or national origin.
   b. religious groups are required to hire members of other religions.
   c. Japanese-American restaurants would be required to hire only workers of Japanese ancestry.
   d. employers must hire an equal number of male and female workers.
12. Under the Labor–Management Relations Act,
   a. unions or employers can force a worker to belong to a union.
   b. workers are allowed to participate in illegal work stoppages or strikes.
   c. unions are prohibited from charging excessive union dues.
   d. management may refuse to bargain with the employees' union.

Using What You've Learned

Title: Getting It Straight

Purpose: To expose you to the realities of the career you intend to pursue, by interviewing people who are involved in that career.

Description: Knowing what kind of career you want to pursue (or think you would like, if you're not sure), contact three different companies that hire persons in that field. Because personnel departments may not be able to offer the depth of information you seek, make your contact with the appropriate department head or other person directly involved.

Task: Complete the chart below. Then, answer the questions that follow.

Query	Company A	Company B	Company C
What education/training is required?			
What is the starting pay? salary? hourly? commission?			
What is the maximum possible pay in 3 years? 5 years? 10 years?			
What benefits are offered?			
What possibilities are there for promotions?			
Is additional training/education necessary to qualify for promotions?			
Is relocation ever required? With what frequency? Available if requested?			

Query	Company A	Company B	Company C
What is the length of the normal workday? 8–5? Nights? Is overtime mandatory? If so, how often; is it seasonal? frequent? Is overtime available if desired?			
Is out-of-town travel involved? How frequently?			
What are the primary duties?			
What incidental skills are helpful (ability to speak to large groups, for instance)?			
What percentage of time is actually spent doing the job for which you are hired? (For example, if you are inquiring about a sales job, how much time is spent selling as opposed to processing orders, checking with suppliers, attending staff meetings, writing reports, etc.?)			

Are the pay scale and benefits what you expected?

____

____

____

Do the possibilities of promotion fit in with your concept of what you want your life to be like in 3–5 years? 6–10 years?

____

____

____

____

Are there duties involved that you hadn't considered? How do they affect your outlook about the career? Is an unexpectedly large amount of time spent doing related tasks? Would these tasks be enjoyable or burdensome to you?

Overall, does the job suit your financial goals, life-style, and personal ambitions?

How similar or different were the three companies in terms of their expectations, utilization of the talents you have to offer, and remuneration?

Do you think, after talking with the three company representatives, that you could utilize your skills and training effectively with any company that hires persons in your chosen field?

Did you sense any philosophical incompatibility that would make you think twice about your career choice or be exceptionally careful about the employer you chose to work for?

PART TWO

GETTING WHAT YOU NEED

CHAPTER

3

Creating A Workable Plan

Overview

The information in this lesson will help you develop for yourself a workable **financial plan** that accommodates your income to your present and future goals. This financial plan is the single most important tool in gaining control of your money and your future. You should make it the basis for every financial decision you make.

The three variables everyone has to work with in making a financial plan are their personal needs, their goals, and their financial resources, or income. The key is to analyze each of these variables and break them down into their components. Once you have the components itemized, you can begin to fit them into a workable plan. To develop a financial plan that works for you, you must:

- List your present and future goals and your current and ongoing expenses.
- Set and prioritize your future goals.
- Explore income sources for meeting future goals.
- Keep track of how funds are budgeted to meet goals as they occur.
- Re-examine and revise your plan when necessary.

The Goal Worksheet on page 62 of your text lists immediate and continuing goals that we constantly work to attain. The worksheet contains spaces for inserting the amounts you are currently spending (or setting aside) to meet your needs, as well as projected amounts that you will be spending one and two years from now. The exercise of filling out the worksheet serves several purposes: it helps to provide a clearer picture of your actual current financial situation; it helps you anticipate future goals as your needs change; and it helps you determine what expenses might be modified to supply more spendable dollars in another area.

As you calculate each monthly expense, whether current or anticipated, include within the expense any debt repayment that may be a part of the total expense. Try also to separate from debt payments that portion attributable to interest, and include those interest items under the category "Cost of credit." For example, under "Transportation," you might break out the amount you spend each month for the repayment of a car loan. Part of that monthly amount is interest. So you should list this interest amount under "Cost of credit." Now you can begin to see your transportation expenses in relation to all your other goals.

For the same reason, you will find it helpful to break down many of the items in the worksheet into more specific components. For example, "Shelter" might include rent or mortgage payments, property taxes, property insurance, utilities, maintenance and repairs, renovation and improvements, and appliances and reserves for replacements. Breaking out the expenses this way gives you a better understanding of continuing and one-time expenses.

In making your plan, keep in mind two kinds of goals—immediate and long-term. Your immediate goals have to do with all those obligations, expenses, and basic needs that you must meet to maintain your present life-style. Long-term goals represent what you hope to attain over the years.

There are also two kinds of dollars—Today Dollars and Tomorrow Dollars. Today Dollars are those applied toward meeting current and continuing needs and goals. Tomorrow Dollars are those that, while available today, aren't spent for current needs. These dollars are ones you put away for use tomorrow.

The ability to meet your long-term goals will be shaped largely by your ability to meet your immediate goals. This is because immediate demands affect your discretionary income. **Discretionary income** is the excess money available once the basic needs you identified are met. It is the key resource you can manage now for attaining your future goals. Just how best to allocate this income becomes clearer when you determine the trade-offs between current and future goals.

The Major Future Goals Worksheet on page 68 of the text lists some of the more common goals that individuals and families anticipate. These future goals are not listed in any order of priority; this is for you to determine. If you can add dollar figures to the columns accompanying the goals, even in rough fashion, you'll probably have a better idea about your personal priorities.

Future income sources include savings accounts and other investments, home and life insurance equities, inheritance, borrowing, and such enforced savings as pensions, Social Security, and profit sharing.

At various points, you'll want to tap the income flow in order to have funds to meet your goals as they come up. To do that, you'll need to keep track of your financial condition by periodically calculating your assets, liabilities, and net worth. **Assets** are the sum of everything you own, plus everything owed to you. **Liabilities** are debts—everything you owe. **Net worth** is the difference between the two.

The whole idea of making a plan is to chart a course for yourself. And, like those planned for ships at sea, your course may change depending on what the future brings. You may decide to change your priorities for your future goals. Or your income sources may change. If you have a plan, it's relatively easy to readjust your match of income and goals. The key point to remember is that when something does come along to alter either your goals or your income, you need to re-examine your plan to see how to accommodate the change.

Learning Objectives

When you complete this lesson, you should be able to:

- □ Identify and discuss the important personal financial expenditures an individual faces throughout life.
- □ Recognize the relationship between immediate and future financial goals.
- □ Describe the various sources of income that can be used to meet expenses.
- □ Explain how personal financial statements are used to assist the consumer in financial planning.
- □ In an equation format, illustrate with figures the relationship among assets, liabilities, and net worth.

Reading Assignment

Read Chapter 3 of the text, "Creating a Workable Plan: Goal Setting and Budgeting," pages 58–79.

Key Terms and Phrases

- ☐ **Assets**—The total value of everything you own, plus everything owed to you.
- ☐ **Discretionary income**—Extra money available once one's basic needs have been paid for.
- ☐ **Liability**—A debt; an amount of money owed to someone else.
- ☐ **Net worth**—The difference between assets and liabilities; a measure of one's wealth.

Self-Test

1. A key element of any personal financial plan is how to distribute income to best accomplish current and future needs.
a. true
b. false

2. Aside from the interest you pay on a home mortgage, the cost of credit should not be considered as a major current expense. Such expenditures are usually of short duration and are therefore insignificant.
a. true
b. false

3. Providing funds for your children to attend college should not be a major concern in your future planning, since federal financial aid programs are available to meet this expenditure.
a. true
b. false

4. Borrowing allows you to accomplish immediately goals that might otherwise take years.
a. true
b. false

5. Since financial statements reflect one's financial condition on a given day, they become valuable only when compared to past statements.
a. true
b. false

6. Basically, equity and the net worth of an asset have the same meaning.
a. true
b. false

7. Of the following current and ongoing expenses, which one would probably require the most dollar outlay?
a. charity
b. insurance
c. clothing
d. shelter

8. Which of the following terms refers to the dollars available after the expenses for your basic needs have been met?
a. discretionary income
b. fixed income
c. investment income
d. retirement income

9. Current and continuing goals are generally met through use of which of the following sources of income?
a. borrowing/credit
b. equities in real property

c. income from work
d. investments

10. Equity can also be referred to as
    a. a liability.
    b. the ability to borrow.
    c. a gift.
    d. a share of ownership in an asset.
11. Net worth is
    a. the sum total of everything you own.
    b. the sum total of the amount you owe.
    c. the difference between what you own and what you owe.
    d. the sum total of your credit obligations plus the value of your assets.
12. If you paid $8,000 for a car two years ago, it has depreciated in value to $5,000, and you owe $3,000 on the loan, what is your equity in the car?
    a. $2,000
    b. $3,000
    c. $5,000
    d. $8,000

Using What You've Learned

Title; Planning a Budget

Purpose: To expose you to current living expenses by preparing a budget.

Description: Calculate the estimated yearly expenses that might be encountered by the typical American family of four, two adults and two children, ages 6 and 9, who live in your community. Most of the information that is requested can be acquired. Assumptions are made:

1. Both adults are self-employed professionals.
2. Members of the family are normally healthy.
3. The family has paid for all furniture and appliances.
4. The family owns two cars: one is fully owned; the other requires a $120 monthly payment.
5. The family must purchase all life and health insurance needs.
6. They live in an $85,000 ranch house with a monthly mortgage payment of $550.
7. The family is an average American family with a $30,000 annual income and tastes and habits similar to yours.

Task I: Considering the above information, complete the following table by providing actual or estimated yearly figures.

A. Shelter		
Mortgage payment of $550/month	$ ______	
Property taxes on $85,000 house	______	
Maintenance estimate	______	
TOTAL SHELTER		$ ______

B. Food		
52 weeks @ $ ______/week	$ ________	
TOTAL FOOD		$ ________
C. Transportation		
Car payment of $120/month	$ ________	
Operation of 2 cars @ $.20/mile for 24,000 miles	________	
TOTAL TRANSPORTATION		$ ________
D. Utilities		
Heat (gas)	$ ________	
Cooking (gas)	________	
Washing machine (gas)	________	
Clothes dryer (gas)	________	
Electric	________	
Telephone	________	
Water	________	
TOTAL UTILITIES		$ ________
E. Insurance		
House ($85,000 value)	$ ________	
Hospitalization	________	
Auto	________	
Life	________	
Mortgage	________	
TOTAL INSURANCE		$ ________
F. Clothing		
Adults:		
New purchases	$ ________	
Maintenance	________	
Children:		
School clothes	________	
Play clothes	________	
Dress and play shoes	________	
TOTAL CLOTHING		$ ________
G. Recreation/Vacation		
Adults: one night out/month for dinner	$ ________	
Children: two nights/month, fast foods and movie	________	
Vacation: one week in Disneyland, Florida, flying	________	
TOTAL RECREATION/VACATION		$ ________
H. Charity		
Religious	$ ________	
Community	________	
TOTAL CHARITY		$ ________
I. Spending Money		
Adults	$ ________	
Childrens allowances	________	
TOTAL SPENDING MONEY		$ ________

J. Education		
Two graduate courses at local college	$ ________	
Music lessons for child	________	
Dance lessons for child	________	
Repayment of parents' student loans	________	
TOTAL EDUCATION		$ ________
K. Medical		
Annual checkups:		
Adults	$ ________	
Children	________	
Dental	________	
Eye care	________	
TOTAL MEDICAL		$ ________
L. Savings		
Savings of $______/month	$ ________	
Retirement payroll deduction of $______/ month	________	
College fund for children of $______/month	________	
TOTAL SAVINGS		$ ________
M. Miscellaneous		
Tobacco (one regular cigarette smoker)	$ ________	
Haircuts, beauty parlor	________	
Pets (one dog)	________	
Hobbies:		
Adults	________	
Chldren	________	
Gifts:		
Birthdays, weddings, etc.	________	
Holiday seasons	________	
Other:		
________________	________	
________________	________	
________________	________	
TOTAL MISCELLANEOUS		$ ________
Summary of Expenditures		
A. Shelter		$ ________
B. Food		________
C. Transportation		________
D. Utilities		________
E. Insurance		________
F. Clothing		________
G. Recreation/Vacation		________
H. Charity		________
I. Spending money		________
J. Education		________
K. Medical		________
L. Savings		________
M. Miscellaneous		________
TOTAL		$ ________

Task 2:

Assume the family has to reduce their budget expenditures by 20 percent because of an emergency. List below the items in the budget that could be reduced or eliminated. Support each reduction with the rationale for your decision.

Item	Amount	Rationale

CHAPTER

4

The Smart Shopper

Overview

It may come as a surprise to you, but your shopping habits can affect your financial status. In fact, if you can improve on your buying habits, you could be better off by $1,000 or even more every year.

Every day you are bombarded with hundreds of advertising messages: on television, radio, and billboards; in newspapers, magazines, and the mail. These messages can encourage bad habits by motivating you to spend dollars that might otherwise have been put to better use. However, your worst shopping habits are a result of your own impulses and unwillingness to take a few extra moments before or during each shopping decision to pick the product that can satisfy your needs at the best possible price. By developing good shopping habits, you can acquire satisfaction at minimum cost. In this lesson, you will learn some smart shopper techniques:

- □ How to save on your food and pharmaceutical expenses.
- □ How to look great without spending too much at the clothing store.
- □ How to get the best value for your money when shopping for furniture, appliances, and other big-ticket items.

Food and Pharmaceutical Expenses

First, let's examine some techniques that can be employed at the supermarket, where the majority of a normal shopping budget is spent. These techniques include using unit pricing, comparing the cost of generic-label goods, avoiding costly convenience foods, using cents-off coupons, and shopping for specials.

Unit pricing can help you decide what quantity of a product is the most economical. **Unit pricing** means calculating the price of a product by the unit of quantity (ounce, pound, etc.) rather than by the container it comes in. Often, a larger quantity is more economical per unit, even though the overall price is higher.

When you compare the price of brand labels versus generic labels, you realize that you can also reap substantial savings by buying generic brands, if you're satisfied with the quality of the products. **Brand-name products** are those items sold by regional or national firms whose names are familiar to us through advertising. These companies spend large amounts of money on marketing and advertising the product and the brand name, and those costs are passed on to you, the shopper. **Generic products** are privately labeled for specific stores or chains of stores. In many cases, the quality of generic products is equal to their brand-name counterparts. What's different about generic products is that very little money is spent on marketing and advertising, and that saving is passed on to you.

Generic products also offer considerable savings in the drugstore, on both nonprescription and prescription items. Ask your doctor if there is a generic equivalent for drugs prescribed or ask the pharmacist to check with your doctor before filling the prescription.

You can also save money by avoiding costly convenience foods. Some tests comparing the use of convenience foods to foods that must be prepared from scratch revealed that convenience can be expensive, not altogether satisfying, and not even time-saving. The only rule of thumb that can be proposed is to compare the do-it-yourself method with the convenience-food approach and determine whether the convenience is worth the price difference.

Other shopping tips that will assist you in stretching your shopping dollars include:

- Buy in bulk. Many stores offer substantial savings if you buy in bulk quantities. In addition to the other discounts you can obtain, buying in bulk quantities protects you against inflationary price increases on those products.
- Use coupons. If you take the time to collect cents-off coupons from the newspapers and magazines on products that you regularly buy, the savings can amount to dollars per week.
- Don't shop when you're hungry. If you do, you're more likely to load up your basket with nonessentials.
- Plan in advance. Follow a shopping list if you want to keep your budget in line.
- Avoid snack foods. They tend to be costly and low in nutritional value.
- Watch how the shelves are stocked. The better bargains tend to be on the lower shelves.
- Look for the thrift shelf. Day-old breads, pastries, and produce, or slightly damaged nonconsumables can represent a substantial saving.

Clothing and Accessories

There is little argument that the well-dressed and well-groomed person enjoys certain advantages over the poorly groomed or slovenly dressed person. Appropriate clothing and accessories can be considered an investment in one's social and business well-being. However, excessive spending on clothing will not necessarily produce commensurate results. So, you must strike a balance between the desired appearance and the cost of creating that appearance. Budget-balancing suggestions include:

- Avoid falling prey to flattery. Shop around for comparable items before you make a decision.
- Embellish a few simple outfits with attractive accessories, as opposed to buying more decorative and more costly basic units.
- Check the advertising in your local newspapers and go where the good buys are.
- Buy clothing and accessories off season when they are usually on sale.
- Consider buying seconds. The usually have only minor flaws and can be priced well below an otherwise identical item.
- Check the cleanability and durability of a garment.
- Beware of counterfeit designer clothes that may be inferior to the genuine article.
- Know the store policy for refunds and returns.
- Since children often outgrow clothing before it has a chance to wear out, it may be false economy to buy top-of-the-line clothing for them.
- You can often get tax dollars back by giving away used clothing.

Furniture, Appliances, and Other Big-Ticket Items

Your overall budget can be drastically affected by the purchase of major home furnishings: furniture, carpeting, and appliances. In weighing your housing/furnishing needs, consider the permanence of your housing arrangement and the age of the occupants. Since tastes do change, it can be foolhardy to choose furnishings that are highly personalized with respect to either design or color.

In shopping for furniture, use great care. Don't guess on color or size. Shop at a number of stores before you make any decision and, at each store, ask a salesperson to go over points about construction and upholstery. Be sure to ask about guarantees and how long they are in effect. Find out if the dealer will deliver and set up the furniture at no extra charge.

In buying bedding, a general consensus of consumer testers is that quality pays. You may save money by buying bedsprings and mattress items that are similarly constructed but do not have matching covers.

The possibilities and price ranges of carpeting and other floor covering are limitless. Personal taste, budget, durability, and cleanability must all be taken into account when choosing floor covering.

What you need, what you like, and what you can afford in appliances are up to you. But before you purchase any appliance, ask about installation, service, and warranties.

When you are ready to purchase furnishings and appliances, be particularly careful of stores with easy-credit terms. The credit may be costly indeed. Compare the financing terms a dealer might offer to the terms available at banks and savings and loans in your area. For buyers with no credit or credit problems, it might be far cheaper to obtain a cosigner for credit purchases rather than become involved with high-interest-rate lenders that ply their wares at the "easy-credit" emporiums.

Learning Objectives

When you complete this lesson, you should be able to:

- □ Identify some of the primary causes of poor shopping habits.
- □ Explain how unit pricing can assist in good shopping.
- □ Compare brand-name products to generic products.
- □ List the advantages and disadvantages of buying in bulk.
- □ Analyze the selling strategy behind the promotion of coupon specials.
- □ List and discuss at least three good buying habits that should be used when purchasing clothing; when purchasing major home furnishings.

Reading Assignment

Read Chapter 4 of the text, "The Smart Shopper," pages 80–100.

Key Terms and Phrases

- □ **Brand-name products**—Regional or national name products that are familiar because of advertising.
- □ **Convenience foods**—That classification of foods that have been fully or partially prepared and usually just have to be defrosted or heated before being served.
- □ **Generic products**—Grocery, pharmaceutical, and other items with "plain" or nonbrand labels.
- □ **Unit pricing**—The pricing of food and other grocery products expressed in units of measure (ounces, pounds, etc.), that is, the price per ounce.

Self-Test

1. Impulse buying in response to advertising is generally a wise approach since advertised goods are usually less expensive than their unadvertised counterparts.
   a. true
   b. false
2. Calculating the price of a product by the ounce is called unit pricing.
   a. true
   b. false
3. It is possible for a generic-name product to be equal in quality to its brand-name counterpart.
   a. true
   b. false
4. Buying in bulk is useful primarily because it allows the consumer to purchase products of better quality.
   a. true
   b. false
5. Convenience foods are more expensive than the do-it-yourself foods because most of the preparation has already been done.
   a. true
   b. false
6. Although buying basic outfits at end-of-season clothing sales can save money, in the long run, the consumer loses because those clothes will be out of style the following season.
   a. true
   b. false
7. Which of the following statements regarding unit pricing is most accurate?
   a. Unit pricing generally demonstrates that brand-name products are less expensive than generic products.
   b. Unit pricing makes it easier for the consumer to compare the values in different-sized containers.
   c. Unit pricing requires that the larger-sized container be the better buy.
   d. Unit pricing is not a practical tool to use when comparison shopping because the average shopper finds it too confusing.
8. Which of the following terms refers to products that are nationally known because of advertising and general familiarity?
   a. brand names
   b. blue-chip names
   c. store names
   d. generic names
9. Which of the following is commonly an advantage of convenience foods?
   a. indefinite storage life
   b. time saver
   c. less expensive purchase price
   d. superior quality over nonconvenience foods
10. Supermarkets and manufacturers use coupon offers
    a. to motivate consumers to try a new product.
    b. to get rid of slow-moving products.
    c. to force shoppers to buy products they normally would not buy.
    d. to make customers happy so that they will come back to the store.

11. The smart consumer purchases
  a. clothing that is basic and simple, and accessorizes outfits attractively.
  b. designer clothes.
  c. decorative and costly outfits.
  d. only brand-name clothes.

Using What You've Learned

Title: Comparing Brand Names and House Brands for Ingredient Content.

Purpose: By examining a product's ingredients, listed on the package, you will realize that the same ingredients are contained in both the brand and generic products.

Description: This project involves a trip to the supermarket and supplying the information requested on the following table.

Task: Complete the table; then, answer the questions that follow.

Product	Size	Cost per Package	Cost per Ounce or Unit	Ingredients	Percent Savings per Ounce for House Brand
Contac Cold Capsules					
House-brand cold capsules					
One-A-Day Brand Multiple Vitamins					
House-brand multiple vitamins					
Philadelphia Brand Cream Cheese					
House-brand cream cheese					
Purina Dog Chow					
House-brand dry dog food					
Tide Detergent					
House-brand laundry detergent					
Wesson Vegetable Oil					
House-brand vegetable oil					

What is your reaction to the information you have gathered? How will this exercise alter your supermarket shopping habits?

____

____

____

____

____

____

Find five other name-brand and house-brand products that have identical ingredients.

Product	Ingredients
1.	
2.	
3.	
4.	
5.	

CHAPTER

5

Frauds and Swindles

Overview

"There's a sucker born every minute," said P.T. Barnum. And the statement is as true today as it was in his time. Despite all the consumer-education materials available, there is still an abundance of shady, misleading, and illegal business going on in every community every day. This lesson will explore some of the more common types of consumer fraud.

In any kind of transaction, you must be aware of certain basic patterns that may indicate a fraudulent setup: the offer of a deal that sounds too good to be true, the sale of an item that is supposedly unavailable through normal channels, inducements so tempting that you may find yourself on the verge of spending money for something you might otherwise have ignored.

Some frauds and swindles are so common that they have acquired names:

Bait and switch is probably the oldest game of all. A clever salesperson diverts you from the bait item, an advertised special, and switches you to another item that offers higher profit. Bait-and-switch tactics are outlawed by the Federal Trade Commission as well as by many state and local laws.

A distinction should be made between bait and switch and "loss leaders." A **loss leader** is a product offered by a merchant at a lower than normal price to entice you into the store where, it is hoped, you'll buy other merchandise as well as the loss leader. Supermarkets and discount stores frequently use loss leaders, and there's nothing wrong with this practice if you are getting the goods as represented and not a cheap replacement.

When you respond to an advertisement, you have time to think about the wisdom of doing so. But when you're confronted by a stranger on the street, the surprise element alone can be enough to embroil you in a money-losing proposition. One such classic scheme is the **pigeon drop.** In a typical situation, the victim is approached by a stranger who indicates he has found a large sum of money, money he or she is willing to share if the victim will put up some money to pay a lawyer. The money left with the con man's "lawyer" disappears quickly, as does the pseudo-attorney.

The **phony-goods scheme** usually starts when you are approached by a stranger on the street offering to sell you anything from watches to perfume. It won't be until after you get home, or until after the salesman has disappeared that you discover that the watch has no innards or that the perfume is kerosene.

In terms of both dollar volume and number of incidents, the U.S. mail is probably the single biggest carrier of fraudulent activity. Mail-order swindles can consist of either an advertisement in print or broadcast form or an advertisement that comes to you in the mail. Either way, you are dealing with unknown people, probably in a different city. If something goes wrong, it is not as easily corrected as it would be if you were dealing with a local merchant. Vanity racket schemes, get-rich-quick promotions, work-at-home schemes, and mail-order merchandise frauds all fall within the category of **mail-order swindles.**

The home is a favorite target for swindlers. Not only are the stakes quite large in **home-improvement frauds,** but the confusion and legal consequences can be devastating. Often the home-improvement pitchman will offer you something too good to be true—work that will last forever and at substantial savings.

To avoid being swindled on a major home-improvement project, do not sign any home-improvement contracts until you have:

- ☐ Prepared or received firm, clear, detailed plans and specifications.
- ☐ Received comparable bids from local reputable contractors based on those plans or specifications.
- ☐ Had the documents checked by an attorney.
- ☐ Discussed with your banker the overall financing of the project.

When it comes to the area of investments, greed and gullibility reach their peak, and the opportunities for fraudulent activities are infinite. The con artist promises instant fortunes and huge tax savings in stocks, commodities, gold, silver, gemstones, land, and virtually anything else that might capture a victim's attention.

If you have been a victim of fraudulent schemes, there's little chance that you'll get your money back unless you're willing to spend a lot of money and time on legal action. Even though the chances of getting your money back are slim, you still should take action if you believe you've been defrauded. If nothing else, your actions may help put a stop to fraudulent practices. The main sources of possible help are the Federal Trade Commission; the U.S. Postal Service; consumer protection offices; newspapers, radio stations, and television stations; Better Business Bureau; and banks, savings and loan associations, credit unions, and consumer finance companies. The small-claims court can be of assistance in settling a claim of fraudulent or improper business practices if you can locate the party who wronged you. Contact your local court to determine their rules and procedures.

Learning Objectives

When you complete this lesson, you should be able to:

- ☐ Define and explain how a bait-and-switch scheme operates.
- ☐ Give an example of at least two mail-order schemes; a fraud perpetrated on homeowners.
- ☐ Discuss why the pigeon drop is such a successful scheme.
- ☐ List three "warning signal" phrases that indicate a probable fraud.
- ☐ Explain how the Ponzi scheme operates and how it relates to the pyramid scheme.
- ☐ Indicate how the Federal Trade Commission aids the consumer in the area of fraud; the Better Business Bureau.

Reading Assignment

Read Chapter 5 of the text, "Frauds and Swindles and How to Avoid Them," pages 101–125.

Key Terms and Phrases

- □ **Advance loan scheme**—A scheme that targets a person in need of money who may have trouble securing a loan through normal channels. A loan is promised if a sizable amount of money—a commission—is paid up front. The commission and the agent disappear long before a loan is forthcoming.
- □ **Bait and switch**—An illegal selling scheme in which a seller offers a product at an unreasonably low price (the "bait"). A would-be buyer, lured by the bait, is then "switched" to a higher-priced item.
- □ **Boiler room**—A fleet of fast-talking, hard-driving telephone salespersons offer a get-rich-quick scheme in a spiel so frenetic it doesn't give the victim time to think. By the time the victim realizes what's going on, it's too late.
- □ **Credit repair clinic**—Unscrupulous clinics promise to help individuals or businesspersons in need of money who might have difficulty borrowing it through normal banking sources. A sizable amount of up-front money is required; all too often it disappears with no benefit returned.
- □ **Loss leader**—A product offered by a merchant at a lower than normal price to lure shoppers into the store.
- □ **Pigeon drop**—A fraudulent activity wherein the victim is persuaded to part with cash in order to share in what appears to be a large sum of money that the perpetrator claims to have found lying on the street. Many variations.
- □ **Ponzi scheme**—A fraudulent investment activity in which new victims are constantly being lured to participate, with their invested money used to pay off prior victims. At some point, the perpetrator attempts to disappear with as much as possible of the victims' money.
- □ **Pyramid**—Closely related to the Ponzi scheme. An investor buys into a scheme and, in order to recoup his or her investment and make a profit, must enlist ten other people, who must each enlist ten other people, and so forth. Pyramid schemes collapse because participants run out of people who are willing to invest and the victims find that their names never move high enough on the list to recoup their (often heavy) investment.
- □ **Time share**—A legitimate concept in which the right to use a resort or hotel facility for one, two, or more weeks per year is purchased. Abuses occur when the promised facilities are not built as promised, are never built at all, are so poorly managed they can't be enjoyed, or the time purchased for exclusive use is sold to others, too.
- □ **Vanity rackets**—Various schemes, sometimes fraudulent, in which the promoter offers to "publish" your book or song, etc., for a fee, no matter what the quality of the work.

Self-Test

1. Because of the impact of the consumer-education effort, the phrase "There's a sucker born every minute" does not apply to the modern consumer.
   a. true
   b. false
2. Most Americans believe that business activities are generally legitimate and that what they are told and read in advertisements is true.
   a. true
   b. false

3. Bait and switch is popular because there are few federal and state laws that make this scheme illegal.
   a. true
   b. false
4. The originator and the participant in a chain-letter scheme are both subject to prosecution under federal postal laws.
   a. true
   b. false
5. In general, the only people who make money on a pyramid scheme are the promoters who start it.
   a. true
   b. false
6. Despite all the promises and guarantees offered by salespeople, would-be investors in precious metals or gems face serious risks unless they obtain independent appraisals of the items.
   a. true
   b. false
7. The purpose of this strategy is to offer the consumer a very low price on a product, with the assumption that they will buy several other products at the regular price.
   a. bait and switch
   b. bulk meat purchase
   c. loss-leader offer
   d. pigeon drop
8. In which of the following schemes is the victim approached by a stranger who offers to share money he has just found?
   a. bait and switch
   b. dump and run
   c. pigeon drop
   d. Ponzi scheme
9. When dealing with a door-to-door home-improvement contractor, the prudent consumer should
   a. insist that all agreements be in writing.
   b. insist on a perfect guarantee.
   c. insist that the contract be signed immediately by the contractor, particularly if it is a "today-only" deal.
   d. check on the contractor's credentials and visit his or her place of business before any contracts are signed.
10. When new investors are constantly solicited and their invested money used to pay off older investments, the practice is termed
    a. a boiler-room operation.
    b. land fraud.
    c. get-rich manual.
    d. Ponzi scheme.
11. During the 1990s, it is predicted that consumers will be subjected to many new fraudulent schemes in the area of
    a. foreign land deals.
    b. home improvements.
    c. precious metals.
    d. stocks and bonds.
12. When a business firm signs a "consent order" with the Federal Trade Commission, the consumer should be aware that
    a. the firm was guilty of some type of fraudulent practice.
    b. the firm has promised not to engage further in a practice which the FTC considers fraudulent.

c. it is unwise to buy any product from such a firm.
d. the consent order is in fact a condemnation of the firm by the FTC.

Using What You've Learned

Title: What to do with Unordered Merchandise Received in the Mail

Purpose: To acquaint you with the procedure to follow if you receive unordered merchandise in the mail.

Description: Assume that you have received the latest edition of "Erotic Art Works of the World." The "art" depicted in the book borders on pornography. The package arrived in the mail. Because it did not have a return address, you were naturally curious and opened it, destroying the arrival wrapper. There was a bill inside for $29.95. Of course, you never ordered this material.

Task: Visit your local post office and describe this hypothetical situation to the postmaster. Obtain the answers to the following questions:

What are the U.S. Postal Regulations regarding the receipt of unordered merchandise through the mail? Can the postmaster furnish you with a copy of the regulations?

Does the postmaster advise you to mail the book back? If so, do you have to pay the postage?

If you keep the book and start to receive credit collection notices from the company, what does the postmaster advise you to do?

Assume that there was a postage-paid return envelope in the package that was to be used to make your payment. Will the post office accept the wrapped book with the postage-paid envelope affixed to the package, so that the company pays the return postage for the book?

In general, what procedure does the postmaster recommend you follow?

____

____

____

CHAPTER

6

Transportation

Overview

"Getting there" used to be no problem in the days before the 1973 oil crisis when cars, gasoline, and mass transit were relatively inexpensive. But today the cost of moving about is a serious matter and must be taken into account in anyone's financial planning. This lesson will help you solve the common problems you face in trying to keep your transportation expenses in line.

The cost of driving cannot be taken for granted any longer. For most it's a major budget item, and an increase or decrease in your driving can have a definite bearing on the rest of your budget. If you are choosing a dwelling or seeking a job, the cost of commuting must definitely be calculated. A 20-mile daily commute can cost $35 per week—$150 per month.

Your overall ability to make ends meet and manage your money prudently requires that you keep your driving to a minimum and that you utilize less expensive transportation (car pooling, mass transit) whenever possible.

In buying an automobile, it is important to distinguish between your automotive needs and your automotive desires. Ask yourself: How big a car do I really need? What optional extras are important? Do I need such frills as power windows, power antenna, power door locks, and the like? A full package of optional extras on a standard car can cost an additional $3,000 or more. For every dollar spent on extras, you'll spend more money on the financing, insurance, and registration, plus extra gas that you'll burn hauling it all around. Optional extras are not a one-time expense; they'll be with you for as long as you own the car.

In dealing with automobile dealers, it's important to remember that the automobile business is extremely competitive. Competitiveness breeds anxiety, and that in turn may cause car salespeople and dealerships to bend the ethics of good business practices now and then in order to win a sale. Generally, there are four types of sales tactics that have brought a poor reputation to a small segment of the automobile sales industry: **highball** and **lowball,** the **takeover operation,** the **bugged room,** and the **disappearing item.** If you spot any of these tactics when you are car shopping, you can be relatively sure that you're in for a high-pressure pitch that might lead you to sign an contract you otherwise wouldn't sign. Awareness of these tricks and a willingness to walk away from shady tactics when you spot them are necessary weapons when shopping for a car.

In negotiating price, there are no rules of thumb, but there are some broad guidelines. Generally speaking, dealers work on a markup of about 20 percent. Thus, depending on the value of your trade-in, whether you're financing through the dealer, and how anxious the dealer is to move his current inventory, it might not be unreasonable to expect a discount of 5 to 10 percent off the sticker price. Consult *Consumer Reports* magazine's annual price listing of new cars for a specific guideline to your bargaining power.

Though some change in traditional patterns has been creeping into the industry, late summer and early fall still tend to be the times when dealers are clearing out their old inventory to make room for the new-model cars. While there may be a smaller assortment of cars to choose from at this time of year, there's a strong chance that you will get a better price than you might have earlier in the model year.

Assuming you have the necessary trade-in or down payment and acceptable credit, most dealers can arrange financing for you right on the spot. You can also make your own financing arrangements through your bank or your car insurance company. It may save you time to have the dealer arrange financing, but it can also cost you money. To find out how much, determine the annual percentage rate (APR) the dealer will charge for the financing. Compare the dealer's APR with that offered by other lenders.

Should you use your old car as a trade-in or sell it yourself? To help you make the decision, first check the used-car price directory and used-car lots to see what cars similar to yours are selling for. If you can find a buyer who's ready, willing, and able to pay the price you establish, it may be wise to make a deal. If you can't find a buyer quickly, and have to advertise extensively, you might be in for more of a headache than the project is worth. Remember that the difference in sales tax may offset any better deal you could get by selling your car on your own. Check in your locality to determine current regulations on this matter.

Also included in your cost of transportation is the expense of maintenance. New-car warranties used to be fairly cut and dried: they were good for 12 months or 12,000 miles, whichever came first. In recent years, however, competition has created a lot of confusion regarding new-car warranties. Many manufacturers now offer limited warranties extending for as long as seven years. But it's important to note that these are limited warranties. The extended warranties generally cover the basic drive train and transmission in the car. Many other items, such as power windows, windshield wipers, radio, dashboard circuits, etc., may still be restricted to the 12 months or 12,000 miles limitation. The matter is further confused by the availability of additional warranties that extend beyond the basic manufacturer's warranty. Some of these plans are offered by the manufacturers themselves, and others are offered by private insurance companies. These extra warranties can cost many hundreds of dollars, depending on the extent of coverage—how many miles and/or how many months they run. Often, the price of these warranties can be negotiated along with the price of the automobile.

An adequate package of automobile insurance protects you against the hazards inherent in owning and using an automobile. The typical insurance policy packages several different types of insurance all together:

- Public liability for bodily injury
- Public liability for property damage
- Medical payments
- Uninsured motorist
- Comprehensive insurance
- Collision insurance

The cost of automobile insurance can vary considerably depending on the age, safety record, and occupation of the owner, and the purposes for which the car is used. Some companies will offer discounts for drivers with safe records and for younger people who have taken certain driver education courses. Other discounts may be available where more than one car is insured and where compact cars are involved. In shopping around for the best protection package, inquire about all available discounts from each agent.

Learning Objectives

When you complete this lesson, you should be able to:

- State the reasons why the cost of acquiring and operating an automobile have increased substantially during the last five years.

- □ Compare the advantages and disadvantages of purchasing a new car; a used car.
- □ List and describe strategies typically used by an automobile salesperson.
- □ Compare the advantages of selling your car versus trading it in.
- □ Explain the importance of knowing the value of your automobile before trading it in on a new car.
- □ Compare the advantages and disadvantages of financing the purchase of a car through a financial lending institution versus the car dealer.
- □ Describe typical car-leasing arrangements.
- □ List and describe the major options available in automobile insurance coverages.

Reading Assignment

Read Chapter 6 of the text, "Transportation: Buying, Financing, and Insuring Your Cars," pages 126–149.

Key Terms and Phrases

- □ **Collision damage waiver**—Rental car companies offer this protection (at a cost of $8 to $12 per day) against responsibility for a deductible of $1,000, $2,000, or more in the event of a collision. For it to be effective, the renter must be using the car in accordance with the strict terms of the rental agreement.
- □ **Collision insurance**—Coverage for the insured's automobile for damages resulting from a collision with another vehicle or object.
- □ **Comprehensive insurance**—Coverage for the insured's automobile for damages resulting from causes other than collision, such as fire, theft.
- □ **Highball**—A selling technique whereby the salesperson attempts to convince you that your property (trade-in car, house) is worth much more than you thought it was in order to lure you into doing business.
- □ **Limited warranty**—A warranty offered by a car manufacturer that is generally limited to the basic drive train and transmission of the car.
- □ **Lowball**—A selling technique whereby the salesperson initially suggests a larger discount off the price of an item than is really possible in order to lure you into doing business.
- □ **Medical payments coverage**—A part of one's automobile insurance (optional) that reimburses driver and occupants for limited medical expenses arising from an accident; also available on homeowner's and tenant's insurance.
- □ **No-fault insurance**—A type of automobile insurance required in some states, in which injured parties are paid by their own insurance companies (up to set limits), regardless of who is at fault in an accident.
- □ **Public liability bodily injury**—Insurance that will provide legal defense and will pay claims if the insured's actions cause bodily injury to others; common with automobile, homeowner's, and tenant's insurance policies.
- □ **Public liability property damage**—Insurance that will provide legal defense and will pay claims if the insured's actions cause property damage to others; common with automobile, homeowner's, and tenant's insurance policies.
- □ **Takeover operation**—A sales technique involving a succession of salespersons, one taking over after the other, at ever-increasing pressure, designed to wear down a customer's resistance, especially in automobile sales.
- □ **Uninsured motorist insurance**—A form of coverage in automobile insurance policies that protects the insured in case of injury in an accident with an uninsured driver.

Self-Test

1. In general, the faster you go, the fewer miles per gallon your car will achieve.
   a. true
   b. false
2. The "dealer's asking price" for a new car is usually inflated to allow for trade-in and customer bargaining.
   a. true
   b. false
3. Late summer and early fall tend to be the best times to buy a new car because dealers want to clear out inventory to make room for new model cars.
   a. true
   b. false
4. Financially, the single most important part of your automobile insurance policy is the public liability coverage for bodily injury.
   a. true
   b. false
5. Should the insured's automobile collide with a telephone pole, he or she would need collision insurance coverage to protect him or her against property damage claims made by the telephone company.
   a. true
   b. false
6. Under no-fault automobile insurance coverage, the insured parties are paid for property-damage expenses and medical expenses, regardless of who is at fault in the accident.
   a. true
   b. false
7. Which of the following should not be considered a major cost of operating your car?
   a. depreciation
   b. gasoline
   c. insurance
   d. the money that you're saving for a new car
8. When the salesperson gives you a sizable discount off the sticker price of a new car, the practice is called
   a. highball.
   b. lowball.
   c. a manager's special.
   d. a manufacturer's rebate.
9. The consumer is most likely to face high-pressure selling in which of the following situations?
   a. highball
   b. lowball
   c. manager's special
   d. takeover operation
10. Which of the following automobile insurance coverage options protects against the damage caused by the insured's automobile to the property of others?
    a. collision
    b. comprehensive
    c. public liability for property damage
    d. uninsured motorist

11. Automobile insurance coverage designed to protect your car against loss from theft is called
    a. collision.
    b. comprehensive.
    c. property damage/loss.
    d. no-fault loss.
12. Insurance premiums for younger drivers are higher because
    a. these drivers have unfavorable statistical records when it comes to accidents and claims.
    b. they usually drive sports cars and tend to speed more.
    c. statistics indicate that young drivers travel more miles and are more likely to be involved in an accident.
    d. they generally drive older used cars which tend to break down more often.

Using What You've Learned

Title: Comparison Shopping for Car Insurance

Purpose: To obtain information from three insurance companies on insurance for your own car. Compare the information, and make a decision as to where to purchase the insurance and which coverage to purchase.

Description: This project requires you to contact three insurance companies to obtain information on the purchase of car insurance. Once you have acquired this information, you are asked to make a decision, with supporting rationale, as to what coverage you would purchase and from whom. Assume you want to insure your own car in the amounts given on the chart below, or substitute the limits of liability and deductibles with amounts of your choosing.

Task: Complete the information requested in the following table, and make a decision as to the insurance you would select, answering the questions that follow.

Coverage	Company A	Company B	Company C
6- or 12-month policy?			
Public liability & property damage limits of liability: 25,000/50,000/10,000 100,000/300,000/25,000 ________________	$________ $________ $________	$________ $________ $________	$________ $________ $________
Medical payments limits of liability: $25,000 $100,000 ________________	$________ $________ $________	$________ $________ $________	$________ $________ $________

Coverage	Company A	Company B	Company C
Uninsured motorists limits of liability: $30,000/$60,000	$________	$________	$________
________________	$________	$________	$________
Comprehensive $100 deductible	$________	$________	$________
$250 deductible	$________	$________	$________
Collision $100 deductible	$________	$________	$________
$250 deductible	$________	$________	$________
Emergency road service	$________	$________	$________
Car rental expense	$________	$________	$________
Death, dismemberment, & loss of sight	$________	$________	$________
Total disability	$________	$________	$________
Loss of earnings	$________	$________	$________
Safe driver or nonsmoker discount?	$________	$________	$________
TOTAL COST	$________	$________	$________
Other Considerations			
Claim service reputation?			
Claims processing time?			
Claims procedure?			
At what point would claims result in an increased premium? What amount or percent?			

Based on the data you collected, which insurance company would you select to handle your policy? Consider the various claims procedures when making your decision; they can vary considerably. A company that has a claims adjustment center where you can drive in, get an estimate, and drive out with the payment in hand could save you time and money. State the reasons for your decision.

If you are sued by someone you injured in an automobile accident and the damages awarded are greater than your public liability coverage, the injured party can go after all your personal assets—your car, home, investments, etc.—to satisfy the judgment. For example, if you have public liability coverage of $25,000, are sued, and the injured party is awarded $100,000, you would be liable for the additional $75,000 and could be forced to liquidate personal assets in order to pay the balance. Would owning a home (vs. renting) make a difference in the amount of public liability insurance you purchase? What other factors would influence your decision?

After examining the types of coverage available and the cost of each, and given the age and condition of your car and your personal financial circumstances, what types of coverage would you carry? If some options are eliminated, explain why. What are your reasons for deciding on the limits of liability and deductibles you selected?

CHAPTER

7

Leisure and Recreation

Overview

The work week is growing shorter—from about 50 hours at the start of this century to about 35 hours currently. Less work time means more leisure time. And more leisure time gives every individual a choice—vegetate or "re-create." This lesson is intended to stimulate you to plan how you can combine your spendable dollars and your spendable future time in the most rewarding way.

Travel agents

A well-trained and experienced travel agent has many tools at his or her disposal to assist you in getting the most out of your vacation dollars. He or she is paid on commission by the airlines, hotels, cruise operators, and tour packagers and will not charge you for services. In some cases, the travel agent may save you money by pointing out off-season bargains or group package tours with itineraries matching your travel plans.

Cruising

The price of a cruise may not be much different from a stay of comparable length at a resort or a moderately budget-wise trip abroad. Like package tours, cruises are advertised on a "from" basis. The price quoted in the advertising is the minimum price for the least desirable stateroom on the ship. Aside from the stateroom, all pasengers have equal use of the ship's facilities, including food and entertainment.

Vacation Tips

Traveler's checks are the best way to carry money with you on a vacation. For a very modest cost, traveler's checks offer a universally acceptable and protected form of exchange: If traveler's checks are lost, the issuing company can arrange for an immediate refund.

If you are traveling in another country, you'll need to convert at least some dollars into the currency of that country for such things as taxis, minor purchases, tips, and the like. Unless you've established a bank account in the foreign country, it will be extremely difficult for you to cash a personal check. Traveler's checks are, again, the best way to carry money.

When booking do-it-yourself travel, it's essential to get all your reservations confirmed in writing from the hotels, car rental agencies, and other facilities you'll be using. Make certain those confirmations spell out exactly what you are getting for your money.

Vacation Investments

If you're contemplating a big-ticket vacation expenditure—such as a van, a boat, or your own home or condo—the best precaution is to proceed on a test basis. Rent for a year or two and see if it's really your style. The rental will probably cost you less than the interest on a purchase and, if you don't like it, you're able to walk away with no obligation.

Time sharing is a recent phenomenon. Simply stated, time sharing means that you buy the right to use a specific apartment, condominium, or resort facility for one or two or more specific weeks a year. Part of the time-sharing concept is that you can exchange your specific location for one of many others each year. It all sounds very attractive. Indeed, the concept is plausible, and some people have found great satisfaction in it. But the time-sharing phenomenon is also rife with misrepresentation and outright fraud. Visit the place in person to be certain it is as it is represented to be. Study your contract carefully to determine what your exchange privileges, if any, might be, and what added costs you might have to incur in the future.

Electronics

As the century draws to a close, virtually every home in America will have one or more of the following: cable television, offering dozens of channels; dish antennas, capable of receiving scores, if not hundreds, of television channels from satellites hovering in space; video player/recorders; wide-screen television sets, five or more feet across; and home computer terminals, capable of interacting with the television for educational, work, and game-playing purposes.

With so many electronic marvels expected in the near future, it can be frustrating to try to anticipate the best investments to make today. But whatever electronic leisure equipment you do decide on will be yours to enjoy for many years, while you plan future investments in more advanced equipment.

Probably the most popular of the new electronic wonders are video cassette recorders. In shopping for a VCR, consider the following: Will you really benefit from the costly optional extras included in many sets, or are you better off with a lower-cost, no-frills set? What type of warranty comes with the set? Parts? Labor? If service is needed, can it be done locally or must the set be sent away to a service bureau? Competition is keen with these products, so it will pay to shop around and seek discounts at local dealers.

The newest technological fad in the home electronic market is the video camera. While the price of a good-quality video camera is on the high side, the cost of capturing images can be much lower than with a camera that uses film. An hour's worth of videotape, in color and with sound, costs less than $10. There are no developing or processing costs. As with all electronic gadgets, technology moves rapidly. This year's best deal may be obsolete almost before you get it home. So, after doing the necessary homework, make your best purchase, and don't look back to see what you might have bought had you only waited another month or two.

The basic component in personal computers is the typewriter-sized home computer, which can be attached to a printer and/or your telephone. The cost of these units ranges from a few hundred dollars to thousands of dollars depending on their capabilities.

Shopping for a home computer and software takes a lot of careful thought. In addition to studying the variety of available equipment, consider whether such a unit will really benefit *your* home. Once you have determined what you need the computer to do, and before you shop for hardware, find out what software is available to perform those applications. Another important consideration for computer units is service. Is service available and easy, and what is the cost?

Large-screen television sets are still expensive, but technological advancement is expected to bring the price down over the coming years. In the meantime, although they can definitely enhance the pleasure you get from watching television, large-screen sets are strictly a luxury purchase.

Personal Enrichment

A great deal of your leisure time can be put to rewarding and productive use without spending much money. Look into the activities that may be available, often at no charge, at your local college, library, church, synagogue, or community center. You're likely to find an assortment of concerts, art exhibits, theatrical presentations, classes, and lectures. Athletic activities, whether individual or organized in teams, are among the most popular of leisure-time activities. Volunteer work—through religious and civic organizations—can also be a rewarding use of your leisure time. Volunteers are eagerly sought and, by helping others, you help yourself.

Learning Objectives

When you complete this lesson, you should be able to:

- □ List the main advantages of using a professional travel agent.
- □ Compare the advantages and disadvantages of package and do-it-yourself tours.
- □ Identify each of the following travel or vacation options: trip insurance, time-sharing arrangements, home-exchange program.
- □ Discuss the advantages and disadvantages of time sharing.
- □ Cite three precautions to take before leaving on a vacation.
- □ Present a prudent rationale for the purchase of electronic home-entertainment equipment.

Reading Assignment

Read Chapter 7 of the text, "Leisure and Recreation," pages 150–171.

Key Terms and Phrases

- □ **Frequent flyer plan**—Most major airlines offer these plans, which enable travelers to accumulate points for distance traveled on a given airline. With accumulated points, the traveler is entitled to either free travel or discounts on future flights.
- □ **Home-exchange program**—A vacation arrangement whereby you swap homes with another party for your vacation period.
- □ **Official Airline Guide (OAG)**—A book available at travel agencies that provides updated information on commercial airline flights. Published monthly.
- □ **Package tour**—A vacation plan that offers one all-inclusive price for your vacation. Usually includes travel, accommodations, sightseeing, services of a guide, meals, and extras.
- □ **Trip insurance**—Insurance that may be purchased to provide a refund if you or a member of your family becomes ill, necessitating cancellation of travel plans.
- □ **Vacation time sharing**—An arrangement whereby you buy the right to use a specific apartment in a resort facility for one or more specific weeks during the year.

Self-Test

1. Although a professional travel agent will assist you in getting the most out of your vacation dollar, the cost of this service is generally higher than the value received, especially for the experienced traveler.

a. true
b. false

2. All or part of the cost of an airline ticket may be nonrefundable if travel plans are canceled before departure.
   a. true
   b. false
3. One of the best ways to stretch your travel dollars is to take advantage of the seasonal bargains available in major resort areas.
   a. true
   b. false
4. Most experienced travelers prefer to arrange their own tours rather than participate in a package tour.
   a. true
   b. false
5. For a very modest cost, traveler's checks offer protection against loss, and are acceptable in most tourist areas.
   a. true
   b. false
6. One disadvantage of a time-sharing purchase is its limitation to the same vacation spot for the same period each year.
   a. true
   b. false
7. Which of the following statements regarding airfares is most accurate?
   a. The fare from city A to city B will be the same for all airlines because of government regulations.
   b. The fare from city A to city B will vary between airlines because of competition.
   c. Airfares will continue to get lower during the 1990s.
   d. Airfares are likely to increase during the 1990s because of reduced competition.
8. Trip cancellation insurance
   a. protects the traveler when package tours are canceled.
   b. insures the reimbursement of money deposited toward a trip in the event the traveler must cancel because of illness.
   c. provides payment to the beneficiary of the insured traveler in case the airplane crashes.
   d. both a and b.
9. A wise strategy to use when arranging for a cruise is to
   a. book the minimum-priced stateroom since most of the time is spent in public rooms and on shore anyway.
   b. book the more expensive stateroom because the quality of the meals and entertainment increases proportionately with the price.
   c. only book on cruise ships that do not require tipping.
   d. only travel on cruise ships that have English-speaking crews.
10. When you buy the right to use a specific apartment, condominium, or resort facility for a specific period during each year, the arrangement is called
    a. home-exchange program.
    b. package tour.
    c. seasonal bargain.
    d. time sharing.
11. One of the major problems facing consumers of electronic home-entertainment equipment is
    a. complicated operating instructions.

b. high acquisition costs.
c. rapid technological changes, which make the equipment obsolete too soon.
d. excessive repair costs.

Using What You've Learned

Title: Let's Go to Hawaii

Purpose: This project provides you with the experience of planning a do-it-yourself vacation and comparing it to the cost of package tours.

Description: Plan an eight-day, seven-night do-it-yourself tour of Honolulu, Hawaii, for you, your spouse, and two teenage children. You will depart from your hometown and stay in a medium-class beachfront hotel. In order to complete this exercise, you will have to obtain several booklets on Hawaii from a travel agent. In addition, you will be required to call the airlines for flight information and prices. If the toll-free number for various airlines is not listed in your directory, call information: 1-800-555-1212.

Task 1: Complete the following table with the actual or estimated expenses for the trip.

Do-It-Yourself Plan

Airfare	
Cost of round-trip airline tickets	
Adults	$________
Children	________
OR	
Family plan	________
Hotel	
Name of hotel ____________________	
Cost of hotel for 7 nights	$________
Tips for baggage handling	________
Ground Transportation	
To airport on departure	$________
From airport on return	________
Airport parking	________
From Hawaii airport to hotel (obtain from airline)	________
From hotel to Hawaii airport (obtain from airline)	________
Tips for baggage handling	________
Sightseeing	
Select any two full-day tours of Hawaii	
Name of tour ____________________	$________
Name of tour ____________________	________

Meals	
Breakfast	$______
Lunch	______
Dinner	______
Snacks	______
Add 15% for tips	______
Adult Entertainment	
Plan on two nightclub shows	
Estimated cost	$______
Other Anticipated Expenses	
________________	$______
________________	______
________________	______
________________	______
Summary of Expenses	
Airfare	$______
Hotel	______
Ground transportation	______
Sightseeing	______
Meals	______
Adult entertainment	______
Other anticipated expenses	______
TOTAL	$______

Task 2:

Take the information you have gathered to a professional travel agent. Tell the agent that you would like to take a trip similar to the one you've planned but wonder if there is a package tour that offers similar experiences at less cost.

Analyze the information the travel agent offers and compare it with your plan. Describe your decision and the reasons for it.

____

____

____

____

____

PART THREE

A ROOF OVER YOUR HEAD

CHAPTER

8

Buying a Home

Overview

A house is the single largest purchase that most individuals ever make, and they generally have to live with it longer than other purchases. A mortgage loan is the biggest debt most people will ever incur, and the monthly cost of the dwelling, including utilities and maintenance obligations, will represent a major portion of most budgets. Each individual or family must decide what will best suit their own specific needs and goals, taking into account all applicable financial, geographical, architectural, and personal factors involved.

Condition of the Dwelling

The physical condition of the premises is one of the most important aspects to be considered in choosing a dwelling. Most of us can tell if walls need painting or if doors and windows close properly or if roof shingles are falling off. But the wise shopper may find it valuable to invest in a professional service that can evaluate the structural and mechanical aspects of the building. Sometimes the condition of the dwelling is covered under a warranty. Unless such warranties are specifically spelled out in a contract and agreed to by the parties, they might not be enforceable. In addition to such warranties, the buyer and seller must agree to clauses concerning specific repairs that should be included in the contract of sale.

Furnishings

Beyond the cost of the house itself, the cost of the money to finance the house, and the cost of the utilities, you must also consider the cost of furnishing and decorating the home you wish to buy. Evaluating such purchases is part of your initial buying decision.

Transportation

Whether you travel by private automobile or mass transit, you cannot afford to overlook the cost involved in getting to and from work, shopping, schools, and other places when you choose a house to buy.

Operating Costs

A generation ago, a home buyer might have paid little attention to operating costs, for they represented a relatively small portion of the total out-of-pocket expense involved in home ownership. Not so any longer. Heating and electrical costs have risen drastically in most parts of the country. Energy conservation is now an economic necessity and must be considered carefully during the home-buying process. The costs of maintenance and insurance have risen and must also be considered.

Price Range

In determining the price range you can afford, you must take into account both the amount of down payment available and the monthly payments. The higher your down payment, the lower your monthly payments, and vice versa.

Before you even begin to look at houses, visit one or more local home financing institutions and determine what they think you can afford. Monthly housing costs for most families will be in excess of 40 percent of their aftertax income. For many families, it may take two incomes to allow them to buy a house.

House Hunting

In addition to scouring the classified ads in your local newspaper and visiting open houses at every opportunity, you should consider the value of finding a good real estate agent to help you in your housing quest. Many people think of using a real estate agent only when they sell a house. But there are many advantages to using a real estate agent when you are buying.

By using the multiple listing service, a real estate agent has access to the vast majority of houses on the market and can help you locate the right house in the right neighborhood at considerable saving in time and energy. A good agent is a skilled negotiator and should be able to help you bargain for the best possible price. And good agents are in constant touch with the financial markets, so that they can help you obtain the financing you'll need. Further, the services of a real estate agent cost the buyer nothing: the agent's commission is paid by the seller.

Your Personal Needs

Layout and size are very practical considerations that the individual or family must weigh in regard to current and future needs. A good price on a house that is too small may prove to be a poor decision if, in a few years, you have either to enlarge the house or to tolerate the inconvenience of inadequate space. Similarly, if a house soon proves to be too large for your needs, you may look back at the original purchase as having been more costly than necessary. Although changes in household size aren't always predictable, the possibilities must be considered.

The Purchase Contract

Traditionally, the seller asks one price, the buyer offers a lower price, and they ultimately settle for something in between. The real estate agent representing the buyer and seller generally conveys the offers and counteroffers back and forth, so that you don't actually come face to face with the seller during the negotiation.

Once you've made an offer and the seller has accepted, the seller's real estate agent usually prepares a brief memorandum of agreement setting forth the basic terms of the deal. The more formal purchase contract, generally prepared by the seller's representative, follows. The purchase contract sets forth the names of the parties involved, describes the property, dictates the terms and conditions of the sale, stipulates the kind of deed the seller will deliver to the buyer, and states where and when the closing is to take place. Only by having your own representative view the document can you be assured that your interests will be fully protected.

Learning Objectives

When you complete this lesson, you should be able to:

- ☐ Describe how financial, geographical, architectural, and personal factors are important considerations for defining housing needs.
- ☐ Explain the difference between a cooperative and a condominium and list the problems that can occur in these housing arrangements.
- ☐ Indicate the considerations involved in determining your housing needs and the price range you can afford.
- ☐ List and discuss the importance of the purchase contract and its major elements.

- ☐ Describe the process of purchasing a house from the time the search begins to the closing date.

Reading Assignment

Read Chapter 8 of the text, "Buying a Home," pages 174–198.

Key Terms and Phrases

- ☐ **Adjustments**—In a real estate transaction, the prorating between buyer and seller of any prepaid expense (such as property taxes) that the seller has incurred prior to the closing.
- ☐ **Closing**—In a real estate transaction, the event at which the transfer of deeds, money, and promises-to-pay takes place.
- ☐ **Condominium**—An owned dwelling unit that is part of a multiple-unit structure.
- ☐ **Cooperative**—A type of housing arrangement wherein each resident owns a percentage of the total building and has an agreement with all the owners for the right to use a specific unit in the building for his or her own dwelling.
- ☐ —Deed—A document by which title to real estate passes from the seller to the buyer.
- ☐ **Earnest money**—A token payment of cash to bind a preliminary agreement between the buyer and seller of a house (or other item).
- ☐ **Easement**—The right given to someone to use your land for a specific purpose (to cross over the property, to construct utility lines, etc.).
- ☐ **Financing contingency clause**—A provision in a contract for the purchase of real estate that allows buyers to be released from obligation if they are not able to obtain financing at a certain rate of interest by an agreed-on date.
- ☐ **Land lease**—An arrangement for purchasing real estate wherein the buyer buys only the structure, and leases the land on which the structure exists.
- ☐ **Lien**—A legal right obtained by a creditor with respect to property that has been pledged as collateral for a loan made by the creditor to the debtor. Having a lien on the property can allow the creditor to force a sale of the property in order to satisfy the debt. Liens against property can also arise as a result of the debtor's failure to pay taxes or failure to pay contractors and artisans who have worked on the property.
- ☐ **Multiple listing**—A service offered by subscribing real estate brokers in a given area, wherein all houses and other properties for sale in that area are listed and described in a frequently published directory.
- ☐ **Restrictive covenant**—A provision in a deed that can control certain things an owner of real estate can or cannot do on the property.
- ☐ **Right of assignment**—A contractual clause that permits a party to a contract to transfer his or her interests in the contract to another party.
- ☐ **Shared housing**—Two or more individuals or families combine their financial resources to purchase a dwelling for themselves.
- ☐ **Title insurance**—Insurance that will reimburse the insured for losses suffered (within stated limits) if a claim is made against the title of property owned by the insured.
- ☐ **Town house**—(also known as row house). A form of dwelling unit adjoined on both sides by similar units.

Self-Test

1. A shared housing arrangement occurs when two or more families or individuals purchase a house and land.
   a. true
   b. false
2. In a condominium arrangement, each resident is responsible only for the property taxes and property insurance of his or her specific unit and not for the taxes and insurance of the common areas of the building.
   a. true
   b. false
3. There is a federal income tax advantage to home ownership in that mortgage interest and property taxes may be taken as deductions.
   a. true
   b. false
4. The advantage of land leasing to a buyer is that the purchase price is lower than it would be had the buyer purchased the land as well as the house.
   a. true
   b. false
5. In a cooperative, each resident owns what is called an undivided percentage of the total building; in a condominium, the resident owns only his or her own specific dwelling unit.
   a. true
   b. false
6. During the 1990s, it is predicted that monthly housing costs for most families will be in excess of 40% of their aftertax income.
   a. true
   b. false
7. A recent death or divorce in a seller's family could be an indication of a good housing buy.
   a. true
   b. false
8. Those factors that include layout of rooms, quality of construction, size, and condition of a house are called
   a. geographic factors.
   b. financial factors.
   c. personal factors.
   d. architectural factors.
9. The legal document used to convey title of property from the seller to the buyer is called a
   a. lease.
   b. deed.
   c. mortgage.
   d. purchase contract.
10. This insurance protects the buyer from monetary damages if a claim is made against the ownership of the property.
    a. mortgage
    b. title
    c. easement
    d. lien
11. The part of a purchase contract that allows a buyer to back out of the contract if he or she cannot obtain financing at an agreeable rate of interest by the closing date is called

a. earnest money clause.
b. mortgage insurance clause.
c. title insurance clause.
d. financing contingency clause.

12. At the time of closing, there are 300 gallons of oil in a 550-gallon tank on the property you are purchasing. If you must pay extra for the 300 gallons, that payment is called
a. a lien on the oil.
b. a restrictive covenant.
c. an adjustment.
d. a financing contingency.

Using What You've Learned

Title: House Hunting

Purpose: This exercise will provide you with exposure to multiple listing services, real estate offices, and agents and with practice in making a decision on purchasing a home.

Description: Complete the following exercise, using data personal to you, or follow the fictitious description.

Assumed you are thirty years old, married with one child, and two more planned. You have an income of $45,000 per year and intend to work in the local income area for the rest of your life. You have $30,000 in savings, which could be applied toward a down payment on a house. Currently, you are living in a two-bedroom apartment and paying $400 in rent and $150 in utility expenses. All assets are owned, including furniture; and you have no outstanding debt.

Task: It is now time to go house hunting. Do the following activities and complete the information requested in the table.

Activity	Requested information
1. At a local real estate office, review a copy of "Multiple Listing Service List of Homes for Sale." Select a house that meets your needs.	1. List the reasons why you selected the house you did. __________ __________ __________ __________
2. Select and visit a real estate agent. Explain the project, the financial resources, and personal givens, and discuss your selection of a house.	2. What was the agent's reaction to your selection? Does it meet your needs?

Activity	Requested information
	Does he or she think you can afford the house?
3. If possible, make arrangements to visit the house with the agent.	3. Was the house representative of the description in the listing booklet? Did it fit the broker's description? List five important things you learned from the visit.
4. If you cannot visit the house, assume that the information about the house is accurate. In order to make a financial decision on purchasing the house, you may find it useful to obtain the additional information requested in the next column.	4. What is your reaction to the neighborhood? What is your reaction to the surrounding houses? How expensive are the monthly operating costs?

Activity	Requested information
	Do you think the house will appreciate in value? ____________________ ____________________ ____________________
5. Based on all the information you now have, make your decision about purchasing the house.	5. Buy ______ or Not ____ List the reasons for your decision. ____________________ ____________________ ____________________ ____________________ ____________________
6. Prepare a brief reaction to this experience.	6. Reaction ____________________ ____________________ ____________________ ____________________ ____________________ ____________________

CHAPTER 9

Financing a Home

Overview

The American dream has long been to own a home. Is the dream now beyond reach? Not necessarily. This lesson will acquaint you with methods of home financing and provide you with the information you'll need to pursue your personal dream of home ownership.

The major sources of home financing are savings and loan associations and mutual savings banks. Many commercial banks also offer home financing plans, as do some credit unions and insurance companies. There are also private mortgage brokers in most communities who act as middlemen in finding mortgage loans for home buyers. They usually obtain the needed funds through institutional or private investors. Mortgage brokers charge a fee for their services; before entering into any commitment with a private mortgage broker, the terms of such an agreement should be understood.

If you're planning to finance a home purchase, you should begin to shop for available financing before you start looking for houses. Talk to various lenders in your community and get an idea of the kinds of financing available to you. Knowing what you can afford makes it easier for you to shop in an appropriate price range and puts you in a better bargaining position with sellers. A seller who is convinced that you are prepared to confirm a deal and that you won't have to wait for weeks to find out whether you can get financing may be willing to lower the price.

A mortgage contains two very important legal commitments. First, you are legally committing yourself to make the payments to the lender as agreed. Second, you are giving the lender the right to take steps to take back the property from you if you fail to make the payments. In other words, you have given the lender a security interest in the property as collateral for the loan.

There are basically two types of mortgage: fixed rate and variable or adjustable rate. In the standard **fixed-interest-rate mortgages,** your interest cost is calculated on the unpaid amount of the debt, or principal balance, at each given monthly point. For instance, on a $70,000 mortgage, set to run for 30 years at a 12 percent interest rate, the monthly payments for interest and principal would total $720. (See table on page 202 of the text.)

Variable-rate or **adjustable-rate clauses** can take many different forms. Be sure to find out the starting and base interest rates, the index that controls the rate, how much the payment can be raised in a given period of time and over the life of the loan, and the possibilities and effects of negative amortization.

One relatively new type of insured loan is the FHA-245, also known as the **graduated payment plan.** This type of loan is geared toward younger people who might not otherwise be able to meet the high monthly payments currently required. For the first few years of the loan, monthly payments are lower than they would be under a regular plan. As the years go by and the borrower's income increases—the assumption on which the plan is based—the payments increase accordingly.

Mortgages may contain clauses that can affect your legal rights as well as your monthly payments. When you sign a mortgage agreement or assume an existing mortgage, you consent to such clauses and give the lender the right to exercise those clauses.

The **balloon clause,** or call privilege, for example, allows the lender to demand that the entire loan be paid, or the interest rate renegotiated, at a given time.

An **assumption clause** in a mortgage means that the owner of a house can sell the property to another party subject to the approval of the lender; and that new buyer can assume the existing debt.

Some mortgages contain **prepayment privileges** clauses that allow you to make advance payments on your debt without suffering any penalty. On the other hand, some mortgages have prepayment clauses stating that you must pay a penalty if you do prepay.

It is wise to spend a few dollars to examine your credit file at the local credit bureau to make sure everything is in order before making your final loan application and before the lending organization conducts its credit check. In addition to obtaining information regarding your credit record, the lender reserves the right to appraise the property you are buying and carry out a title search to assure the security of the loan. These processing steps can take from a few days to a few weeks and may entail some fees that you will be expected to pay whether the loan is approved or not. If your application is approved, you should obtain a copy of the lender's commitment, in writing, so that there is no mistake about the terms of the agreement.

As the price of homes and the cost of financing has increased, a number of creative financing arrangements have emerged. **Creative financing** covers any type of financial agreement a buyer and seller negotiate privately, with or without the participation of outside lenders or investors. In short, the term describes the way in which deals can be made when normal financing programs aren't feasible or available. Examples of creative financing arrangements include land contracts, shared appreciation mortgages, and sleeping seconds. All three could carry risks for the buyer who is not protected legally in the fullest capacity. It is absolutely essential that before you commit yourself to any such technique, you get adequate legal advice. These arrangements can be very complex and create legal pitfalls that you might not be aware of.

Learning Objectives

When you complete this lesson, you should be able to:

- □ Compare the advantages of fixed-rate and variable-rate mortgages.
- □ Describe the major elements of a typical mortgage payment; the various clauses that are part of the mortgage agreement.
- □ List and explain the importance of the three types of insurance generally associated with a house purchase.
- □ Discuss the term "creative financing" and its importance in the purchase of a house.
- □ Select the best mortgage arrangement from among several different financial plans.
- □ Explain how the length of a mortgage affects the amount of the monthly payment and total interest paid.

Reading Assignment

Read Chapter 9 of the text, "Financing a Home," pages 199–220.

Key Terms and Phrases

- □ **Acquisition costs**—Expenses a borrower will have to pay in obtaining a home financing loan. Generally payable to the lender, these expenses can include legal fees, appraisal fees, and points.
- □ **Adjustable-rate loans**—Simply stated, an adjustable-rate loan means that the interest rate can be adjusted up or down over the months and years.
- □ **Annual cap**—An annual cap puts a limit on how much the monthly payment on an adjustable-rate mortgage can increase during a year.
- □ **Assumable mortgage**—A mortgage that allows future creditworthy buyers of the property to take over responsibility for paying the existing plan.
- □ **Assumption clause**—A clause in a mortgage agreement that allows the property owner to sell to another party, who can assume the existing debt.
- □ **Balloon clause**—A provision in a loan agreement (mortgage or installment) that allows the lender to demand full payment of the loan at a set point in time.
- □ **Base rate**—The interest rate on which the lifetime cap on an adjustable rate mortgage is calculated.
- □ **Buying down**—A type of "creative" home financing plan whereby the seller pays part of the interest charges for the buyer for a specific period of time.
- □ **Creative financing**—A general term describing home financing arrangements that are privately negotiated between seller and buyer, with or without the participation of outside lenders or investors.
- □ **Default insurance**—A type of mortgage insurance that guarantees payments will be made for a set period of time in the event the borrower defaults.
- □ **Escrow**—1) A third party who acts as an intermediary in a real estate transaction, seeing to it that the instructions of the parties are complied with. 2) A sum of money paid monthly to a mortgage lender to pay property insurance premiums and property taxes as they fall due. Also referred to as an escrow account, or reserve account.
- □ **First mortgage**—see **Mortgage**
- □ **Fixed-rate mortgage**—A type of home financing wherein the interest rate the borrower pays remains the same over the life of the mortgage.
- □ **Foreclosure**—The procedure by which a lender can obtain title to property that has been pledged as security for a loan when the borrower has defaulted on that loan.
- □ **Graduated payment plan**—A home financing plan that permits the borrower to make lower than usual payments in the first few years, with payments increasing in the later years.
- □ **Index**—An arbitrary number, beyond the control of the lender, used to determine interest rate adjustments on an adjustable-rate mortgage. Common indices are the so-called "cost of funds" for savings institutions in your region or one of a number of different interest rates the U.S. government pays when it borrows money.
- □ **Initial rate**—An attractively low interest rate on an adjustable-rate mortgage designed to lure customers into a given institution. The initial rate will last only until the first interest adjustment occurs, which is usually after six months.

- □ **Land contract**—A manner of purchasing real estate wherein the deed is not conveyed to the buyer at the closing, but rather at some future date, as agreed on by the parties.
- □ **Lifetime cap**—This fixes the maximum interest rate that will can be charged during the life of an adjustable-rate loan.
- □ **Mortgage** (known as **trust deed** in some states)—A debt secured by real estate. When one borrows money to pay for a home purchase, the debt is referred to as a first mortgage, and/or a purchase money mortgage.
- □ **Negative amortization**—A situation that can occur when the annual cap on an adjustable-rate mortgage prevents a lender from charging the prevailing interest rate. When this occurs, the difference between the interest rate being paid monthly and the prevailing interest rate is added back onto the overall debt, resulting in an increasing, rather than decreasing principal balance.
- □ **Open-end clause**—A clause in a mortgage that allows the borrower to borrow back up to the original amount of the loan at the original, or otherwise agreed-on, interest rate.
- □ **Points**—Added fees a lender charges a borrower, usually in a home financing transaction. One point equals one percent of the amount of the loan.
- □ **Prepayment clause**—A provision in a mortgage that determines the extent to which the borrower may make advance payments on a loan and what penalties, if any, may have to be paid as a result.
- □ **Purchase money mortgage**—The basic mortgage whereby one borrows money to purchase property.
- □ **Rate lock**—A guarantee that the interest rate on a loan will not go above a certain level, regardless of the amount of time it takes to complete the transaction.
- □ **Shared-appreciation mortgage**—A form of mortgage wherein the lender charges the buyer a favorable interest rate in exchange for a share in future profits from the sale of the property.
- □ **Sleeping second**—A creative financing tool involving a second mortgage, which will be owed by the buyer to the seller, but on which no payments will be required for an agreed-on time.
- □ **Variable-rate mortgage**—A home financing arrangement in which the interest rate payable by the borrower may fluctuate up or down.
- □ **Wraparound mortgage**—A creative home financing plan in which the buyer makes a single monthly payment to the seller, and the seller in turn makes two or more payments to actual mortgage holders. The "wraparound," in effect, is a form of consolidation of two or more mortgage debts.

Self-Test

1. Since a creative financing arrangement is usually made between the buyer and seller, a simple written agreement can be made, saving the expense of attorney fees.

a. true
d. false

2. A "buying-down" offer is an indication that the seller is anxious to sell the property.

a. true
b. false

3. In the event interest rates go up during the life of a mortgage, financial institutions require that you maintain an escrow (reserve) account to cover the additional interest charges.
   a. true
   b. false
4. If you are 15 days late in your mortgage payment, the financial institution will more than likely start foreclosure proceedings on your property.
   a. true
   b. false
5. When arranging a fixed-rate mortgage, it is important to have a clear understanding of the possibility and effects of negative amortization.
   a. true
   b. false
6. A typical mortgage payment includes a portion for interest and principal reduction and may include an amount for house insurance and property taxes.
   a. true
   b. false
7. The major portion of each monthly payment during the early years of a mortgage is applied to interest owed on the loan.
   a. true
   b. false
8. This clause in a mortgage agreement allows the lender to demand that the entire principal balance be paid off on a specified date.
   a. prepayment clause
   b. acquisition clause
   c. open-end clause
   d. balloon clause
9. A financing plan whereby the monthly payments are low in the first years and increase as the years go by is called
   a. a variable-rate mortgage.
   b. a graduated payment plan.
   c. a fixed-rate mortgage.
   d. an open-end clause.
10. This type of mortgage allows the lender to share in any profit on the property at the time of sale.
    a. sleeping second
    b. purchase money
    c. shared appreciation
    d. adjustable rate
11. A mortgage in which the monthly payments for interest and principal remain the same for the entire length of the mortgage is called
    a. a fixed-rate mortgage.
    b. buying down.
    c. a second mortgage.
    d. a shared-appreciation mortgage.
12. Of the following clauses in a mortgage, which could be favorable to the borrower?
    a. open-end
    b. balloon
    c. foreclosure
    d. prepayment penalty

Using What You've Learned

Title: Shopping for a Mortgage

Purpose: To acquaint you with several mortgage plans currently being offered by local lenders.

Description: This project gives you the opportunity to visit lending institutions and obtain information on available mortgages.

Task 1: Visit the various financial institutions listed below and complete the table.

Institution	Interest Rate	Points	Down Payment	Maximum Length of Mortgage	Special Conditions
Commercial bank					
Savings bank					
Small finance company					
Savings and loan association					

Task 2: Interview one of the officers at the financial institution and obtain the following information.

A. How available is mortgage money?

____

____

____

B. Are interest rates apt to be going up or down in the near future?

____

____

____

C. Will the fixed- or variable-rate mortgage be the arrangement of the future?

____

____

____

D. What advice can he or she give on purchasing a house under today's economic conditions?

____

____

____

Task 3: Based on the information obtained in Tasks 1 and 2, prepare your reaction to the current mortgage market. Is it a good time to buy or should you wait?

CHAPTER

10

Housing Costs and Regulations

Overview

The cost of maintaining a home does not end with writing your monthly mortgage or rent check. Homeowners, or condominium owners in particular, experience an additional drain from such expenses as property taxes, property insurance, utilities, and maintenance. This lesson will assist you in planning for such housing costs. It will also alert you to the legal rights and responsibilities that pertain to housing.

Property Insurance

Choosing the right type and amount of property insurance is important for both homeowners and apartment dwellers. Property insurance provides two forms of protection. First, it provides reimbursement for loss or damage to the physical premises and its contents. Second, it protects you in the event harm comes to others or their property as a result of your negligence in maintaining the property. While you, as a property owner, are not legally required to carry public liability insurance, you are required by law to pay damages if a court finds you responsible for injuries suffered by another on your property.

Both public liability and homeowner's insurance can be purchased from insurance companies. Like other forms of insurance, property insurance is competitive. Rates for the same amount of coverage vary from company to company, and the cheapest premiums may not provide adequate coverage. The only remedy is to consult three or four firms for prices and coverage. You should try to gauge the extent of the services you'll get from the company—how well and how quickly they'll respond to claims—as well as the likelihood that premiums will increase if claims are made.

Valuable personal property such as antiques, coin collections, jewelry, and works of art may *not* be adequately covered for theft or loss under your basic homeowner's or tenant's policy. To assure adequate coverage for loss of these items, you may have to obtain a separate **personal floater.** The cost of this added insurance can be considerable. You must weigh the risk of loss against the added premium.

Your property insurance premium will vary in relation to the deductible you choose. The **deductible** is the amount you pay out of pocket for any losses before the insurance company becomes responsible. Some policies have a no-deductible clause, making the insurance company responsible from the first dollar lost. A $50 deductible means that you must pay the first $50 of an expense in any claim before the insurance company becomes responsible. Deductibles may be obtained for as much as $500. In choosing higher deductibles, you are exposing yourself to greater potential risk in return for a lower premium.

The **coinsurance clause** in your policy can be extremely important. It states generally that if you wish to receive full replacement value for any damage to the premises, you must insure it for at least 80 percent of its replacement cost. If you are not insured to this extent, the insurance company will pay in proportion to the percentage for which you are insured.

As a homeowner or tenant, it is important for you to inventory your furnishings, appliances, and personal property periodically and evaluate the current market or replacement costs of those items to know whether you are adequately covered. Many policies offer clauses that automatically increase the amount of coverage in line with inflation. If you acquire new property or dispose of old items that have been insured, you must notify the insurance company so that the new acquisition can be properly covered and the old dispositions properly deleted. When the insurance company is notified of any change, it issues an endorsement amending the policy. This endorsement should be attached to the policy itself.

In the event you suffer loss or damage, notify your insurance agent immediately. Delay in reporting could jeopardize your rights under your homeowner's policy. Even if you don't think the loss is covered, you should discuss the matter with your agent. You might be pleasantly surprised.

Property Taxes

Owners of all nonexempt property are required to pay property taxes in return for which the city provides services. In theory, the residents of each city decide the amount and type of services they want. City officials determine what type of property will carry what share of the overall tax burden, and evaluate each property in the city. When the current value of every property is known, the **assessment rate** is applied. For example, a city may determine that residential property will be assessed at 20 percent of market value, while commercial property will be assessed at 25 percent, and industrial property at 30 percent. All properties of the same type with equal market values are assessed equally.

Once the assessment rates are established, the city officials look at expenses, determine how much money is needed, and establish the tax rate. For example, they may establish a tax rate of $100 for each $1,000 of assessed value. Thus, a home with a current value of $60,000 will have an assessment value of $12,000 (20 percent of the current market value) and will pay property taxes of $1,200 for the year ($100 for every $1,000 of assessed valuation). The tax rate is adjusted annually to balance city income and expenses as closely as possible. Local laws provide measures by which property owners can protest the assessment on their property and, if successful, reduce the assessment and thereby the taxes.

The owner of a house must also make arrangements with local utility companies to provide gas, electric, water, and telephone service. The individual owner will be responsible for paying for these utilities. In addition to the hints and tips that utility companies publish from time to time, they may be willing to send a representative to examine your home to see how you might be wasting energy. Such an inspection can result in money-saving suggestions.

To the homeowner, a periodic property inspection is an important defense against major maintenance expenses. In addition to taking care of repairs before they become major problems, the wise homeowner should establish a reserve fund for repairs and replacements. Having this reserve allows the homeowner to take care of these costs without having to interfere with borrowing lines, savings accounts, or the regular budget.

Learning Objectives

When you complete this lesson, you should be able to:

- □ Differentiate between the three primary forms of homeowner's insurance: basic, broad, and comprehensive.

- ☐ Explain the importance of, and complications involved in, tenant's insurance.
- ☐ Define the coinsurance clause, and indicate how it works.
- ☐ Discuss the procedure for filing a claim against a homeowner's policy.
- ☐ Relate the assessment rate and assessed valuation to property tax determination.
- ☐ Describe the proceedings for appealing an assessed valuation.
- ☐ Explain how zoning affects home ownership; the law of eminent domain.

Reading Assignment

Read Chapter 10 of the text, "Housing Costs and Regulations," pages 221–236.

Key Terms and Phrases

- ☐ **Assessment rate**—A percentage of the market value of a parcel of real estate, used to establish the property taxes on that parcel.
- ☐ **Basic form homeowner's insurance**—An insurance policy that protect the homeowner against the most common risks involved in owning a home.
- ☐ **Broad form homeowner's insurance**—An insurance policy that includes the same coverage as the basic form and provides protection against additional risks for an extra cost.
- ☐ **Coinsurance clause**—A provision in most property insurance policies stating that the insured party will receive full replacement value for losses if the premises are insured for a stated percentage (usually 80 percent) of full value.
- ☐ **Comprehensive form homeowner's insurance**—An insurance policy that combines both the basic and broad forms, generally referred to as the "all-risk" policy. Certain risks may still be excluded: earthquake, tidal waves, sewer backups, landslides, floods, war, and nuclear radiation.
- ☐ **Eminent domain**—A legal concept that permits a local government to acquire, or condemn, private property when a proven public need for the property exists, such as widening a highway or building a school. Owners of private property must be adequately paid for their property.
- ☐ **Tax rate**—With respect to real property taxes, the factor used to determine the amount payable, usually expressed in terms of dollars per $1,000 worth of assessment value; a tax rate of $20 per $1,000 applied to property assessed at $40,000, will result in an annual property tax of $800.
- ☐ **Zone**—A specified area within a community that can be used only for specified purposes, such as residential, commercial, etc.

Self-Test

1. The assessed value of your property should be used to fix the fair market value for the purpose of determining how much insurance protection is needed.
   a. true
   b. false

2. You do not have to insure the value of your land because, theoretically, land cannot be destroyed.
   a. true
   b. false
3. To assure full benefits, the coinsurance clause requires that the insured have coverage for a certain percentage of the value of the property.
   a. true
   b. false
4. The cost of homeowner's insurance can be decreased by increasing the deductible amount.
   a. true
   b. false
5. Privately owned property can be acquired by the government for use as a public park under the law of eminent domain.
   a. true
   b. false
6. The typical homeowner's policy can provide for medical expenses (within the policy limits) resulting from injury to visitors to the insured's property.
   a. true
   b. false
7. Renters need not be concerned about purchasing insurance to cover their personal property as it is insured under the property insurance carried by the owner of the premises.
   a. true
   b. false
8. Legally, it is possible to reclassify an agricultural zone to a residential zone.
   a. true
   b. false
9. A comprehensive homeowner's policy will usually not cover losses due to
   a. an oil burner explosion.
   b. lightning.
   c. floods.
   d. theft.
10. The amount of property taxes you pay on your property is determined by
    a. the Internal Revenue Service.
    b. a local tax assessor.
    c. a local tax collector.
    d. the amount of insurance you carry on the property.
11. Which of the following is not a factor on which homeowner's insurance policies are based?
    a. the type of property being insured
    b. the amount of liability coverage required
    c. the amount of the most recent property tax bill
    d. the number of risks covered
12. If a neighbor falls and breaks his leg while on your property, the lost earnings suffered by the injured party will be reimbursed under what clause of your homeowner's policy?
    a. public liability
    b. comprehensive
    c. will not be covered by homeowner's insurance
    d. by the neighbor's homeowner's policy

Using What You've Learned

Title: Does Your Homeowner's Policy Cover These Situations?

Purpose To analyze a comprehensive homeowner's policy in relation to the risks covered.

Description: Obtain a copy of a comprehensive homeowner's policy. Examine the policy, or visit with your insurance agent, to determine the coverage in each of the following instances.

Task: Examine the policy and determine if the situations described in the following table are covered.

Situation	Covered? Under What Clause?	Amount Covered	Evidence Needed to File Claim
Your home is 50% destroyed by fire			
A tree is hit by lightning and falls on an unattached storage shed on your property. It is completely destroyed. Is the shed covered? Is the value of the tree covered? Is the cost of the cleanup covered?			
Your dog bites a neighbor's child. The medical bills amount to $150.			
You leave the washing machine on while you go shopping. When you return, you find that the hot-water hose has broken and water has ruined your $4,000 wall-to-wall carpeting.			
The babysitter you hired burns herself on the stove while making lunch for your children.			
The fire insurance company charges you $100 to put out a small brush fire on your property, which someone else started.			
You are on vacation, and someone steals your luggage from the hotel lobby.			

Situation	Covered? Under What Clause?	Amount Covered	Evidence Needed to File Claim
A raccoon gets into your swimming pool and tears the plastic liner.			
Your son hits a baseball and breaks a valuable antique vase.			
The mailman trips on your steps. His medical expenses amount to $1,000, and he is out of work for six weeks. He sues you for $5,000 for lost pay and his suffering.			

CHAPTER 11

Renting

Overview

Millions of Americans rent their homes. Many do so because they've not been able to accumulate enough money to purchase a house or condominium. Other simply prefer the freedom and flexibility of renting. In addition to personal choice, there are legal and financial considerations involved in the decision to rent or buy.

One of the advantages of renting is flexibility. When a lease expires, the tenant is free to move or to renew the lease, assuming that tenant and landlord agree to renewal terms. There are none of the time-consuming, expensive concerns of selling one house, buying another, and trying to dovetail the two transactions. For renters of furnished units, there's not even much to move. In addition, renters usually have only a rental deposit tied up in the transaction; a much smaller amount than the down payment, mortgage, and interest homeowners have invested.

On the other hand, home ownership provides income tax advantages not available to renters. Tax laws allow owners to take deductions for the interest they pay on their mortgage and the property taxes they pay. This can mean substantial savings in taxes. Further, if a profit is realized from the sale of a home, that profit, depending on the tax laws that obtain at the time of sale, may be subject to favorable tax laws.

In some cases, the advantages of home ownership may not be as attractive as they seem on the surface. When considering the financial implications of owning versus renting, base your analysis on your own particular tax situation. The numbers will differ from person to person, from deal to deal, and from year to year.

A renter can occupy a dwelling either on a month-to-month basis or on a fixed-term basis. On a month-to-month basis, boht the landlord and the tenant have the right to terminate the arrangement after giving 30 days' notice to the other party. Commonly, the landlord expects the tenant to comply with certain rules and regulations, which are often spelled out in a written agreement. With a fixed-term agreement, the landlord and tenant agree, in a written document called a lease, to the length, terms, and cost of occupancy.

A lease contains some key clauses that could affect the nature and cost of the occupancy:

- □ the right to privacy and quiet in your home, termed "quiet enjoyment"
- □ who is responsible for what expenses (utilities, painting, etc.) in connection with the property
- □ who is responsible for making and paying for repairs

If you wish to have the right to sublease to another party during your tenancy, make certain that the lease specifies this privilege. A **sublease privilege** gives the tenant the flexibility of being able to move out before the lease has expired and to defray obligations by allowing another party to live in the apartment or house. If you do sublease to another party, you must make certain in advance that the party is creditworthy and reliable, as you are responsible for the rent should the subtenant default, as well as for any damage done.

Not all leases contain renewal privileges. Without a **renewal option,** the landlord can ask whatever rent the market will bear when the original lease term expires. A renewal option protects the tenant; he or she has the right either to stay on at an established rent or to move out. Some leases contain an **automatic renewal clause,** making the lessee responsible for lease payments for an additional term if proper notice is not given.

Virtually every city has ordinances pertaining to health and safety measures in multiple-residence dwellings. These ordinances require landlords to maintain proper levels of sanitation, structural soundness, adequacy of plumbing and wiring, and precautions against fire. If a tenant feels that his or her rights have been violated with respect to these health and safety ordinances, the landlord should be notified.

In some situations, a tenant has the option of purchasing the rental property. A **lease with an option to buy** gives tenants the right to notify the owner of their intent to purchase the property at a price established at the time of the rental. During the period of tenancy, the owner cannot sell the poperty to any other party unless the tenants agree to release their option to buy.

By entering into a lease with an option to buy, the owner of the premises is taking the property off the market for at least the term of the lease. Because there is no assurance that the tenant will purchase the property, the owner can be expected to charge a premium for the lease, and perhaps for the purchase as well.

The conversion of apartment houses into individual condominiums has become a common occurrence, particularly in larger cities. People who have been tenants in a particular apartment for many years may find themselves with the choice of moving out when their lease is up or buying the apartment they have been renting. This can be a hardship for those tenants who must move because they do not have a down payment. On the other hand, some tenants welcome the conversion as an opportunity to convert their nondeductible rent payments into substantially tax-deductible mortgage payments.

Condominium-conversion laws were passed to protect the former type of tenant. These ordinances typically require at least a majority approval of existing tenants before a landlord can convert the property into condominiums and may also require approval of the city.

Learning Objectives

When you complete this lesson, you should be able to:

- ☐ Discuss the pros and cons of renting.
- ☐ Given specific financial and personal information, make a decision as to whether it is better for you to rent or buy.
- ☐ Indicate the income tax implications of renting and buying.
- ☐ Distinguish between the various forms of leases.
- ☐ Compare the advantages and disadvantages of rent-control laws.

Reading Assignment

Read Chapter 11 of the text, "Renting," pages 237–254.

Key Terms and Phrases

- ☐ **Condominium conversion**—The act of modifying the form of ownership of a multiple-unit building from single ownership of the entire structure to individual ownership of each specific unit within the structure.
- ☐ **Equity**—The difference between what your house (or other property) is currently worth and what you owe on it.
- ☐ **Lease**—A contract by which the owner of a property allows a tenant to use that property for an agreed-on time and price.
- ☐ **Lease with option to buy**—At any time during their tenancy, renters have the right to notify the owner of their intent to purchase the property at a previously agreed-on price. The owner cannot sell the property to any other party unless the tenants agree to release their option to buy.
- ☐ **Lease with right of first refusal**—During the period of tenancy, the owner is free to offer the property for sale to others subject to the right of the tenant to meet or beat any bona fide offer the owner may receive.

Self-Test

1. The written agreement between a tenant and landlord is referred to as the lease.
a. true
b. false

2. One of the primary advantages of renting is flexibility.
a. true
b. false

3. Renters generally have the same income tax deductions as homeowners.
a. true
b. false

4. Frequently, homeowners have a better chance to protect themselves against inflation than renters.
a. true
b. false

5. Under strict rent-control laws, rent is more likely to decrease than increase over the long term.
a. true
b. false

6. The freedom to modify your dwelling is much greater if you are a renter than if you are a homeowner.
a. true
b. false

7. A written agreement that gives the tenant the right to purchase the rental property is called
a. a lease with an option to buy.
b. a sublease agreement.
c. a renewal option.
d. an amendable sell lease.

8. Which of the following can protect a tenant against substantial rent increases?
a. rent increase protection insurance
b. failure to comply with quiet enjoyment

c. lease with right of first refusal
d. rent control

9. A tenant may purchase his or her rental unit
   a. if the rent goes up more than 10 percent per year.
   b. under a condominium conversion offering.
   c. under a subowner's agreement lease.
   d. if the landlord breaks the lease.
10. Wihch of the following is considered a disadvantage of renting?
   a. no chance to profit or build equity
   b. flexibility of moving
   c. little or no money tied up
   d. high utility expenses
11. Which of the following would be considered a favorable clause for the tenant in a lease agreement?
   a. a renewal option clause
   b. a security deposit clause
   c. a clause indicating that the tenant pays for all improvements
   d. a 30-day right of landlord to cancel lease clause
12. Under which of the following leases does the tenant have the right to meet or beat any bona fide purchase offer the owner receives during the term of the tenancy?
   a. lease with option to buy
   b. lease with option to sell
   c. lease with a right of first refusal
   d. lease with a renewal option

Using What You've Learned

Title: Making the Decision to Rent or Buy

Purpose: The object of this project is to acquaint you with some of the pros and cons of renting vs. buying and relate those factors to your personal financial situation, life-style, and goals in making the decision to buy or rent.

Description: Assume you have money enough to make a down payment on a house or condominium and are in a position to choose between buying and renting.

Task: Using the points to consider below as a guide, chart the advantages of each, given your personal likes and dislikes, life-style, and goals, and decide which option you would choose.

Ownership Considerations	Rental Considerations
□ large monetary investment: down payment	□ security deposits the only money that is tied up
□ equity increased through monthly payments	□ no equity resulting from monthly payments
□ property likely to appreciate in value	□ no investment advantage
□ income tax advantage	□ no income tax advantage
□ increased income over time vs. relatively stable monthly payment	□ rental payments likely to keep up with increased income/inflation

Ownership Considerations	Rental Considerations
□ cost of maintenance your responsibility (next year's vacation money may be needed to install a new heating system)	□ maintenance expenses not your responsibility (no worry that emergency repair will put you in debt or use up your "fun" money)
□ time investment necessary for yard/ house upkeep; or monetary investment to hire gardener, painter, etc.	□ free time is your own since upkeep is usually taken care of by owner or landlord
□ advance planning for time spent away from home: arrange for lawn to be mowed, plants watered, house to look lived in to minimize vandalism potential	□ minimal preparation needed to spend time away from home: uninterrupted outside maintenance; greater sense of security from proximity of neighbors in multiple-unit dwelling
□ freedom to modify, decorate, and improve home as desired	□ limited freedom to decorate, modify, improve home to suit yourself
□ permanency; but relocation complicated, costly	□ ease of relocating

Your Personal Perspective

Advantages of Owning	Advantages of Renting

Weigh the overall pros and cons, and decide which option you would select.

____

____

____

Would your decision be different if you decided from a strictly financial perspective? from strictly life-style preference? If so, does condominium ownership (financial advantages of owning; outside maintenance attended to by others) offer a viable alternative to you?

____

____

____

Does your career or job situation influence your decision? In what way?

If you are not in a position to consider buying right now, did this exercise help you to decide if home ownership is a goal you want to work toward?

CHAPTER 12

Selling Your Home

Overview

Perhaps the only transaction more complicated than buying a house is selling one. Indeed, many people find themselves doing both simultaneously. When selling a house, or even when vacating leased premises, there are so many personal details to attend to that important financial aspects of the matter can be overlooked. Such oversights can be costly. This lesson will explore how to obtain the maximum resale value on your property.

If you're already committed to a new dwelling, and feel that you must sell your home by a certain date or risk having to make two payments, time can be a costly pressure. Under the crush of a deadline, you are likely to accept a lower price than the house might otherwise bring. And you're liable to make other mistakes, financial or legal, that you could later regret.

Does it pay to use a real estate agent to sell your home, or should you try to sell it on your own and save the commission fee? If time is no object to you as a seller, you might want to try, for a limited time, to sell it on your own. If you haven't received any acceptable offers within a reasonable length of time, it might be best to turn to real estate professionals for assistance. A good agent can help you in

- marketing and pricing your home
- advertising
- showing your home
- listing your home in a multiple listing directory
- financing
- negotiating

Generally, the real estate agent will state what commission he or she expects to receive, but it can be worth your while to negotiate for a lower commission. If it appears that the house will be easy to sell—because of its condition, location, asking price, or other factors—the agent might be willing to accept a lower commission.

If you want to sell your home as quickly as possible and at the best possible price, it may be worth spending some money and energy putting the house in the best possible condition to attract and convince buyers. Consider the following:

- **The exterior.** The exterior appearance of the house and grounds—landscaping, exterior paint, and general upkeep—is vitally important. If there are signs that indicate that the exterior of the house hasn't been maintained, a prospective buyer might well suspect that there are problems lurking inside as well.
- **The interior.** A would-be buyer entering your home should get the impression it is bright and cheery, light and airy. Try various combinations of natural and artificial light to achieve the best effect for each room. The kitchen may be the most important room to many potential buyers. Do what you can to make it sparkle.
- **Touching up.** Any buyer examining a house will constantly be thinking, "How much will I have to spend to put the place in the kind of shape we want it to be in?" Your real estate agent can help you determine where touching up might improve the sales potential of the house.

- **Closets and storage space.** Cluttered closets, basements, and attics discourage buyers. Before you begin showing the house, scour these areas thoroughly. Get rid of everything you don't need.
- **Mechanicals.** Make sure everything works properly: electrical circuits, light switches, plugs, doorbells, plumbing, windows, furnace, air conditioning, and so on.
- **Design.** Examine the major rooms in the house to see how minor changes of furniture or lighting might improve the room's appearance. You might be able to enhance the appearance of the house with throw pillows, scatter rugs, and other decorative pieces that can be acquired at reasonable prices.
- **Leaks and other damage.** If a leak exists, get it corrected. If nothing else, the sign of a leak gives a would-be buyer a better bargaining position.

If you sell your home at a profit, that profit may be subject to income taxes in the year in which you sell. If you sell your property and suffer a loss, the loss is not deductible. But there are important tax provisions that can allow you to postpone payment of taxes or eliminate them altogether. There are two types of tax breaks that can benefit property sellers:

- **The rollover.** The rollover is available to sellers of any age. If you sell your home at a profit, the tax on the profit may be postponed if you buy and occupy another principal residence of equal or greater cost within 24 months rom the date of sale. (Check current tax laws; such provisions are subject to change.)
- **The exclusion.** The exclusion is available only to sellers aged 55 or over. If you or your spouse is 55 years of age at the time you sell your home for a profit, you can exclude up to $125,000 worth of profit from taxation altogether. In order to qualify for this exclusion, you must have owned and occupied the house as your principal residence for at least three of the five years preceding the date of sale.

The exclusion is a once-in-a-lifetime privilege. The rollover can be used over and over again, until such time as you sell your home and do not purchase another one. At that time, the taxes will become due on all aggregate profits realized in prior years.

Whether you're buying or selling a house, you're going to be moving. The decision to hire a moving company or do it yourself will probably depend on the number of household goods you'll be moving, the distance, and the time of year.

If your relocation is job-related, a major portion of the moving expenses not reimbursed by your employer may be tax-deductible. In order to deduct moving expenses, you must meet two tests: the distance test and the work test. The distance test does not refer to the location of your new residence, but rather to the location of your new place of work and its distance from your old and new places of residence. To pass the work test, you must be employed full time for at least 39 weeks during the 12-month period immediately following your move.

Tax counsel is advisable before you undertake your move to alert you to all possible expenses that might be deductible in accordance with specific Internal Revenue Service regulations in effect at the time.

Learning Objectives

When you complete this lesson, you should be able to:

- List and discuss those factors that should be considered when establishing the selling price of a house.

- □ Explain how a real estate agent can assist you in selling a house.
- □ Describe those preparations and property repairs that will assist an owner in selling a house.
- □ Explain the federal income tax alternatives available for handling the profit on the sale of a house.
- □ Discuss the complications involved in terminating a lease.
- □ Indicate the factors that should be considered in selecting a moving company.

Reading Assignment

Read Chapter 12 of the text, "Selling Your Home," pages 286–304.

Key Terms and Phrases

- □ **Exclusion**—That portion of profit on the sale of a house that is free of income taxes. For example, if the seller of a home is over the age of 55, he or she may be able to exclude from taxable income up to $125,000 worth of profit on the sale of a home.
- □ **Listing contract**—A contract between a seller of real estate and a real estate broker, in which the seller gives the broker the exclusive right, for a specific period of time, to try to sell the property.
- □ **Rollover**—Postponement of taxes otherwise due on a profit from sale of a house when the seller buys another house of equal or greater value within two years.
- □ **Take back paper**—Expression that applies to a situation in which the seller of property accepts the buyer's IOU instead of cash. The IOU will be secured by a mortgage on the property; also referred to as "take back a mortgage."

Self-Test

1. If your neighbor has recently listed his or her house for sale at $140,000, you can be assured that your house is also worth a similar amount.
   a. true
   b. false
2. The possibility of selling your house quickly, and at the price you are asking, will increase if you are willing to take back (or carry) the mortgage.
   a. true
   b. false
3. The real estate agent is usually better qualified than the owner to show a house to prospective buyers.
   a. true
   b. false
4. The local board of realtors sets the commission rates that real estate agents can charge, and therefore they cannot be negotiated.
   a. true
   b. false

5. In general, the kitchen is one of the most important rooms to prospective buyers.
   a. true
   b. false
6. One of the disadvantages of selling a house is that the seller must always pay capital gains tax on the profit of the sale.
   a. true
   b. false
7. Which of the following terms describes the technique whereby capital gains tax on the profit from selling a house can be postponed?
   a. take back paper
   b. deferred assumable
   c. rollover
   d. creative taxation
8. The real estate agent's commission for selling a house is
   a. paid by the seller.
   b. paid by the buyer.
   c. divided equally between the buyer and seller.
   d. paid by the mortgage company.
9. This federal tax implication concerns people 55 years of age and over who sell their home:
   a. exclusion
   b. loss or reduction of Social Security benefits
   c. lowballing
   d. deed of trust
10. When selling a house, which of the following may be tax-deductible?
    a. loss on the sale
    b. gain on the sale
    c. expenses of renting while attempting to sell
    d. moving expenses
11. The agreement that permits a real estate agent to offer your house for sale is called
    a. lowballing.
    b. a lease.
    c. an exclusion.
    d. a listing contract.
12. You can generally establish a better selling price for your house if you
    a. offer a rollover advantage to the buyer.
    b. eliminate the listing contract.
    c. offer the buyer the services of a real estate agent.
    d. offer an assumable mortgage.

Using What You've Learned

Title: Finding the Right Movers

Purpose: This project will provide you with the opportunity to investigate and evaluate moving companies and their practices.

Description: You are selling your four-bedroom furnished house in New York and are moving to California. The contents of your house are valued at $40,000. This project involves investigating three moving companies and selecting the company best suited to move your house contents.

Task:

Contact three interstate moving companies. Complete the following table, answering the questions that follow.

Information	Company A	Company B	Company C
Is the company under the jurisdiction of the Interstate Commerce Commission?			
How is price determined: by weight? volume? length of move?			
What is the price of packing and of packing cartons?			
Is insurance included in price? what amount? additional coverage recommended?			
What other services are included in price? What additional services are available, and at what price?			
How long will it take to transport your belongings?			
Contact local consumer affairs office or Interstate Commerce Commission and ask them if any complaints have been filed.			
What other information will aid you in making your choice?			

Based on the information you have gathered, make a decision as to the moving company you would hire. Support your decision.

____

____

____

PART FOUR

WHERE THE MONEY IS

CHAPTER

13

Financial Institutions

Overview

Until the early 1980s, there was a clear distinction among the various types of financial institutions. Commercial banks specialized in checking accounts, business loans, and consumer loans. Savings institutions focused on savings plans and home financing. Stock brokerage firms bought and sold stocks, bonds, and other types of investments. Insurance companies specialized in life insurance products, pension arrangements, and annuities.

Within a decade these distinctions began to blur, and a number of giant financial "supermarkets" had become realities.

Financial institutions play an important "middleman" role in the nation's economy and in your own personal financial situation. They provide a safe depository for those with excess funds to invest. At the same time, they supply services and loans at a fair and reasonable cost. There are many different kinds of these financial institutions.

Commercial banks are referred to as "full-service" institutions. They offer a broad range of services, including checking accounts, savings accounts, trust facilities, and virtually all types of loans. The 15,000 commercial banks in the United States may be chartered by the state or federal government and are generally limited to doing business within their state boundaries.

Mutual savings banks are few in number (about 360 located in roughly one dozen states), but they are substantial in size, controlling almost $160 billion in assets. Mutual savings banks are state-chartered. The major part of their business includes savings plans and loans on real property—mortgages and home-improvement loans. Deregulation in the financial industry, though, has allowed mutual savings banks to expand their scope of business to include checking accounts and various types of consumer loans.

Savings and loan associations number about 3,200 throughout the nation. Like commercial banks, they may be either federally or state-chartered. Traditionally, savings and loan associations concentrated their business in savings plans and home loans, but the era of deregulation has given them powers to offer checking accounts and various consumer loans.

Credit unions are nonprofit, tax-exempt associations operated solely for the benefit of their membership: individuals who work for the same employer or have another common bond. Credit unions accept savings accounts and may pay slightly higher interest than other institutions. This is possible because they are not profit-motivated, are generally located in very modest quarters, and do not have to pay any federal income taxes. Credit unions in some areas may make loans to their members at more favorable interest rates than elsewhere. In recent years, credit unions have also gained the authority to offer a form of checking account.

The following financial services are commonly found at larger commercial banks. They may also be available at smaller banks, savings and loan associations, mutual savings banks, and credit unions.

- □ checking accounts
- □ savings accounts
- □ safe deposit boxes
- □ trust departments
- □ installment loans
- □ credit cards
- □ business loans
- □ mortgage loans
- □ special checks
- □ notarial services
- □ electronic banking
- □ collection services
- □ international banking
- □ investment departments

Companies and individuals who perform financial planning services—called financial planners—are a new type of financial institution that has emerged in recent years. Some are independent. Some are associated with insurance, brokerage, and accounting firms. Some perform services on a fee-only basis. Some earn commissions from products (insurance policies, mutual funds, etc.) they sell to their clients.

The swift rise of financial planning as a profession has been accompanied by an equally swift rise in abuses. Throughout most of the nation, there are few laws governing or licensing financial planners. Virtually anyone can call himself or herself a financial planner, with or without credentials, education, or scruples. If a consumer gets involved with an unscrupulous so-called planner, there will probably not be any governmental agency with which to register a complaint or any recourse for lost money.

The distinction between checking accounts and savings accounts has been blurred in recent years. Formerly, checking accounts did not pay interest; only savings accounts did. Now we have checking accounts that pay interest and savings accounts that allow check-writing privileges. The important matters to consider in shopping for the best account are the minimum balance you're required to keep in the account in order to earn interest and offset service charges, the number of checks you customarily write each month, and the overall convenience you can enjoy and relationships you can establish by dealing with a particular institution.

Three types of savings accounts are generally available at commercial banks, mutual savings banks, savings and loan associations, and credit unions: passbook accounts, certificates of deposit, and money market accounts. The old standard type of savings account is the **passbook account,** which may be opened with any amount of money, and deposits or withdrawals made as desired. In contrast, the **certificate of deposit** is a contractual agreement between customer and institution, whereby the customer agrees to leave a certain sum of money on deposit for a fixed period of time. Certificates of deposit generally pay a higher rate of interest than passbook accounts because the institution is assured that it will have the fixed sum of money available for lending for a known period of time.

Money market accounts are, in a sense, like a super passbook account. They pay a higher rate of interest than passbook accounts but usually require a fairly substantial initial deposit—perhaps $1,000 or more. As a general rule, you can make deposits to, or withdrawals from, a money market account as desired. Many such accounts impose a service charge if there are too many deposits or withdrawals in a given period of time.

Although **direct loans** will be covered in Lesson 14, you should be aware that loans are a key bank service. In addition to direct loans, banks offer some **indirect loans** like credit cards. Whenever you charge a purchase to a bank credit card, you are receiving a loan from the bank. The bank actually pays the merchant for you, and you don't have to pay the bank until the next statement arrives. That's a loan. It's an interest-free loan as long as you pay all that is due to the bank at the end of each month. However, most issuing institutions require an annual fee for the use of the charge card.

Safe deposit boxes, another service of financial institutions, provide the best security for valuable items and documents that cannot be replaced or duplicated. Financial institutions that have safe deposit facilities make boxes of varying sizes available, generally on a yearly rental basis. The person renting the safe deposit box must sign a signature card at the time of rental. In addition to the signature identification, it takes a combination of two keys—one held by the customer and one held by the institution—to allow entry to the box.

Trust departments are usually found in larger commercial banks. The basic function of a **trust department** is to act as a custodian of money or property for customers. The financial institution is responsible for investing the money prudently, for managing the property, and for selling any securities or properties it deems proper to sell.

In addition to the above services, most financial institutions are also a source for the purchase of traveler's checks and money orders.

Learning Objectives

When you complete this lesson, you should be able to:

- □ Discuss the advantages and disadvantages of doing business with the various types of financial institutions.
- □ Describe how a checking account works and list the advantages of its use.
- □ Recognize those situations in which a consumer should use blank, restrictive, and special check endorsements.
- □ Explain the importance of understanding a bank's check-clearing policy.
- □ Describe the procedure for stopping payment on a check and list situations where it might be used.
- □ Perform a checking account reconciliation.
- □ Differentiate between a regular passbook savings account and a certificate of deposit.
- □ Define and explain the purpose of the Fair Credit Billing Law, Fair Credit Reporting Law, Equal Credit Opportunity Act, the Fair Debt Collection Practices Law, and the Truth in Lending Law.

Reading Assignment

Read Chapter 13 of the text, "Financial Institutions," pages 274–306.

Key Terms and Phrases

- □ **Blank endorsement**—A type of check endorsement whereby the payee simply signs his or her name on the back of the check. The most dangerous type of endorsement because, once executed, the check becomes a bearer instrument and can be cashed by anyone in possession of the check.

- **Cash management account**—A type of account offered by stock brokerage firms that provides a combination of checking, investing, and borrowing capabilities.
- **Cashier's check**—A check drawn on a bank's own account.
- **Certificate of deposit**—A contractual investment with a financial institution wherein the investor agrees to deposit a fixed sum of money for a fixed amount of time in return for a guaranteed interest rate.
- **Certified check**—An individual (or business) check that has been guaranteed by the bank on which it is drawn; that is, the funds are guaranteed to be available when the check is presented for payment.
- **Credit union**—A type of financial institution that is owned by individuals who have a common bond, such as the employees of a company or governmental agency.
- **Equal Credit Opportunity Law**—A federal law designed to prevent discrimination regarding sex or marital status of individuals applying for credit.
- **Fair Credit Billing Law**—A federal law that protects the rights of persons who receive erroneous bills from creditors.
- **Fair Credit Reporting Act**—A federal law that gives individuals the right to view their credit history, and the right to take steps to have errors corrected.
- **Fair Debt Collection Practices Law**—A federal law that protects debtors from unfair, deceptive, and abusive debt collection practices.
- **Federal Deposit Insurance Corporation (FDIC)**—The federal agency that insures accounts in commercial banks and mutual savings banks against the failure of the institutions.
- **Federal Savings and Loan Insurance Corporation (FSLIC)**—The federal agency that insures accounts in savings and loan associations against the failure of the institutions.
- **Financial planners**—Companies and individuals that perform financial planning services.
- **Money market account**—A type of savings account that pays a higher rate of interest than passbook accounts but usually requires a fairly large initial deposit. Deposits and withdrawals can generally be made as desired although many institutions impose a service charge if there are too many transactions within a stated period.
- **Negotiable order of withdrawal (NOW) account**—A form of checking account that pays interest to the account holder.
- **Overdraft**—The result of writing a check on one's checking account when the amount of the check exceeds the balance in the account.
- **Reconciliation**—The procedure by which one ascertains whether his or her checking account balance matches the bank's calculations.
- **Restrictive endorsement**—A type of check endorsement that restricts what can be done with the check; usually used in a "deposit-only" situation.
- **Special endorsement**—A type of check endorsement used when the owner of the check (payee) endorses the check to a third party.
- **Stop-payment order**—Written instructions to a bank, given by the maker of a check, ordering the bank not to pay a specific check that the maker has issued.
- **Truth in Lending Law**—A federal law that, among other things, requires lenders to provide a uniform interest-rate equation to borrowers.
- **Usury laws**—State laws that dictate the maximum rate of interest that can be charged for various types of loans.

Self-Test

1. Credit unions operate solely for the benefit of their members and should not operate on a profit basis.
   a. true
   b. false
2. A check containing a blank endorsement can be cashed by anyone who is the bearer or holder of it.
   a. true
   b. false
3. A personal check that has been certified indicates that the check has not yet been cleared for payment by the financial institution.
   a. true
   b. false
4. The Truth in Lending Law fixes the maximum interest rate that can be charged on loans by financial institutions.
   a. true
   b. false
5. Under the Equal Credit Opportunity Law, when a husband and wife apply jointly for a loan, the account must be opened in the name of the spouse who earns the most money.
   a. true
   b. false
6. Under the Fair Debt Collection Practices Act, a financial institution may not employ a debt collection firm to collect on delinquent loan payments.
   a. true
   b. false
7. One of the main differences between a commercial bank and savings and loan is that the latter
   a. does not have insurance to protect its savings account customers.
   b. does not offer checking accounts.
   c. concentrates on making loans for home purchases or improvements.
   d. concentrates on making loans to big businesses.
8. This type of financial institution does not accept savings deposits and offers loans only to the public:
   a. credit union
   b. mutual savings bank
   c. commercial bank
   d. small finance company
9. This instrument is drawn on a bank's own account and guarantees that the funds will be available when the check is presented for payment.
   a. cashier's check
   b. certified check
   c. personal check
   d. traveler's check
10. This process involves bringing your checkbook balance into agreement with the bank's statement balance for your account:
    a. certification
    b. clearing
    c. drafting
    d. reconciliation
11. A law that dictates the interest ceilings that can be charged for various types of loans is called

a. the Equal Credit Opportunity Law.
b. the Monetary Decontrol Law.
c. the Truth in Lending Law.
d. a usury law.

12. A federal law that allows you to have access to your credit history file, maintained by your local credit bureau, is the
    a. Equal Credit Opportunity Law.
    b. Fair Credit Billing Act.
    c. Fair Credit Reporting Act.
    d. Fair Debt Collection Act.

Using What You've Learned

Title: Comparison Shopping for a Passbook Savings Account

Purpose: This project will acquaint you with the types of passbook savings accounts offered at various financial institutions and how they differ in interest rates and services.

Description: You will be required to contact at least two of each type of institution or pick up printed information brochures available at these institutions and use the information you obtain to complete the table that follows.

Task: Complete the table, and answer the questions that follow.

Considerations	Commercial Bank			Savings & Loan			Mutual Savings Bank			Credit Union		
	A	B	C	A	B	C	A	B	C	A	B	C
Interest rate												
How compounded?												
How figured? on high balance? low balance? average balance?												
Penalty for excessive account activity?												
Does the account entitle you to other services? traveler's checks money orders safe deposit box notary services credit card loans 24-hour teller open Saturdays other												
Are deposits insured?												

Using $1,000 as a basis of calculation, assuming this full amount will be maintained in a savings account for a full year, and selecting institutions that utilize different methods of computing interest, calculate the interest that would be earned in that year at at least two of the financial institutions you surveyed.

How do the various institutions compare in terms of interest rates and services offered? Did you find them surprisingly similar? Different? Given the comparative information you gathered in this survey, do you think it is worth the time spent to shop for other banking services, such as loans, checking accounts, and certificates of deposit?

Are the "extra" services offered at the various banks of importance to you? Would you make use of them if they were available? How much influence do these services have in your decision?

Which institution have you decided to establish an account with? What are your reasons?

CHAPTER

14

Credit and Borrowing

Overview

Credit—the ability to borrow—is not a right. It's a privilege, earned through careful planning and faithful performance. Credit needs are those various needs that can or must be fulfilled through borrowing: the purchase of an automobile, home improvements, personal emergencies, the use of revolving charge accounts.

Your **credit capacity** is the amount of borrowing you can realistically handle, given the bounds of your present income and other expenses and your anticipated future income. By consulting a lending officer every two or three years to review your access to credit, credit needs, and credit capacity for the present and near future, you can make the most satisfying and economical use of credit.

One common source of credit is the **installment loan,** available at banks, savings and loan associations, credit unions, and consumer finance (small loan) companies. As a general rule, the cost of borrowing tends to be highest at the consumer finance companies. Interest rates at credit unions may be equal to, or less than, at banks and savings and loan associations.

When you purchase such items as automobiles, furniture, and appliances, the dealer may be able to arrange financing for you. The dealer may extend the loan to you directly or place it with a financial institution.

Charge accounts are also used as sources of credit. Department stores, for example, approve "open-end" credit arrangements with creditworthy customers. This allows you to charge purchases up to a certain limit at these stores, leaving your cash resources for other needs.

Credit cards have become one of the most popular sources of credit. The most common types are those offered by banks and savings and loan associations: MasterCharge and VISA. The so-called travel and entertainment cards (American Express, Diners Club, Carte Blanche) are commonly used for business purposes at hotels and restaurants. Airlines and gasoline companies also issue credit cards for use in obtaining their specific products and services.

Any lender, that is, any potential source of credit, will attempt to determine if you are an acceptable risk before issuing credit. The usual source of information for a lender is a credit bureau. **Credit bureaus** exist in every community; they gather information on the credit performance of individuals in their area. These performance records are known as an individual's **credit history** and are used by potential lenders in their decision-making. The Sample Credit Bureau Report, Figure 14-1, on page 312 of the text shows what a typical credit report looks like.

The fee, or rent, you pay for the use of someone else's money is called **interest.** Interest rates are expressed as a percentage of the amount borrowed for a given period of time. For example, if you borrow $1,000 for one year, and the interest rate is 10 percent per year, you will pay a fee of $100 (10 percent of $1,000) for the use of the money. If you borrow $1,000 and the interest rate is expressed as 1 percent per month, you will pay $10 per month (1 percent of $1,000 is $10), or total interest for the year of $120. In these examples, you have the use of the entire $1,000 for the full term of the loan, whether that is one year or one month. This kind of interest is known as **simple interest.**

Prior to the passage of the Truth in Lending Law in 1969, a borrower could be easily confused or misled by the manner in which interest rates were quoted. A borrower requesting a loan might be told that the interest rate was 10 percent but not whether that 10 percent would be calculated as simple, add-on, or discount interest. Under the Truth in Lending Law, lenders and grantors of credit may calculate their interest rate and other finance charges in any way they want within the limits of the state usury laws. But, no matter how those rates are calculated, they must be expressed in terms of **annual percentage rate,** or APR.

The down payment you make on any purchase you intend to finance will affect the amount of interest you pay and therefore the total cost of the item. The less you borrow, the less total interest you'll be paying, and the lower your monthly payment and overall obligation. (Table 14-4 on page 321 of the text, "Effect of Down Payment on Loan Costs on a $3,000 Purchase," illustrates this point.) Thus, the larger the down payment, the better. This is particularly true if loan interest rates exceed the interest that your savings account might earn if you left some of the down payment in your savings account.

The amount of time, or the term, of an installment loan can also affect overall costs considerably. The longer the term, the lower the monthly payments and the higher the interest costs. (See Table 14-5 on page 322 of the text, "The Effect of Different Terms on Loan Costs.") Generally speaking, the life of the loan should not exceed the expected life use of the product or service you purchase. Also, when you borrow for a recurrent need, such as an automobile or taxes, the loan should be paid in full before the need recurs.

Prior to 1987, virtually all the interest you paid on non-housing-related loans could have been deductible on your tax return if you itemized deductions. The Tax Reform Act of 1986 gradually phases out the deductibility of consumer interest so that, by tax year 1991, there will be no deduction allowed. The cost of borrowing money is greater than it previously has been because of the loss of this deduction.

Many lenders suggest that you obtain credit insurance as a part of your installment loan transaction. If you obtain credit insurance against health disability, the insurance company will make your payments on the loan if you become disabled for an extended period of time. A credit life policy will pay any remaining balance on a loan if the borrower dies before the loan is paid off. While these policies are appropriate in some situations, they do add to the cost of the loan.

As much as the wise use of credit can enhance your life, the abuse of credit opportunities can be very harmful. Some of the more common credit abuses include:

- **Pyramiding.** This occurs when one loan is added to another before the first is paid off. If a car is financed for four years and traded after three, and the new car financing is added to the unpaid balance of the old car, that is pyramiding.
- **Ballooning.** A balloon payment is a large payment that is due at the end of the loan term. If the borrower isn't prepared to meet the large payment, it may be necessary to refinance that payment and incur additional interest costs.
- **Loan consolidation.** This involves taking out a new loan to pay off a number of smaller debts, a practice that means additional interest payments in the long run. In many cases, if the borrower can manage to continue payments until some of the smaller loans mature, the pressure will ease, and the rest of the loans can be paid with less difficulty.

Borrowers who anticipate a delinquency problem should talk with creditors, in person if possible, before payments are missed and explain the circumstances. It may be possible to arrange alternate payment dates or secure a temporary reduction in payments. It may even be possible to have late charges waived.

Learning Objectives

When you complete this lesson, you should be able to:

- □ Describe the procedure for refinancing an installment loan and indicate the advantages and disadvantages.
- □ Relate the size of the down payment on a loan to the total interest paid and the size of the monthly payment.
- □ Illustrate the following credit abuses: pyramiding, ballooning, oversecuring, and loan consolidation.
- □ Compare the advantages and disadvantages of declaring individual bankruptcy.
- □ Describe the two basic bankruptcy proceedings available to individuals.

Reading Assignment

Read Chapter 14 of the text, "Credit and Borrowing," pages 307–337.

Key Terms and Phrases

- □ **Add-on interest**—One method of calculating interest costs on an installment loan. Example: if you borrow $1,000 for one year at 10 percent add-on interest, the interest cost, $100, is "added on" to the amount borrowed, making the total debt $1,100. Dividing by 12 results in monthly payments of $91.67.
- □ **Annual percentage rate (APR)**—The interest rate that the federal government requires lenders to disclose to borrowers in most installment loan transactions. The APR is designed to offer an accurate comparison of interest costs on different loan offerings.
- □ **Balloon clause**—A provision in a loan agreement (mortgage or installment) that allows the lender to demand full payment of the loan at a set point in time.
- □ **Bankruptcy**—Federal court proceedings in which the debts of individuals or companies can be wiped out or in which the court may instruct creditors to hold off in their attempts to collect debts due them from the bankrupt person or company.
- □ **Cosigner**—One who jointly signs a credit agreement with the principal borrower. The cosigner must pay the debt if the borrower fails to do so.
- □ **Credit bureau**—A nongovernmental organization that collects and distributes credit information. Merchants and lenders use this information to make decisions on granting credit to those who apply.
- □ **Credit capacity**—The amount of borrowing a consumer can realistically handle, considering his or her income and expenses.
- □ **Credit health insurance**—A form of health insurance that will pay loan payments if an insured borrower is disabled because of health or accident.
- □ **Credit history**—The record of an individual's credit activity, as maintained by the local credit bureau.

- **Credit life insurance**—A form of life insurance that will pay off any balance due on an installment loan if the borrower dies before the loan is otherwise paid.
- **Debt counseling service**—An agency that assists creditors who are having financial troubles.
- **Discount interest**—A method of calculating interest costs in an installment plan. Example: if one signs a loan agreement for $1,110 for one year at 10 percent discount interest, the interest cost, 10 percent of $1,110, or $111, is "discounted," or subtracted, from the total IOU, leaving the borrower with $999 cash. Dividing $1,110 by 12 results in monthly payments of $92.50. (Compare add-on interest.)
- **Down payment**—That portion of the purchase price (of a house, car, etc.) paid by the buyer in cash at the time of purchase.
- **Interest**—The fee paid for the use of another's money.
- **Loan consolidation**—A procedure whereby one new loan is obtained and the proceeds are used to pay off numerous smaller loans.
- **Pyramiding**—A form of credit abuse, largely self-inflicted, which occurs when a loan taken for a recurring purpose (car purchase, vacation) is not fully paid by the time the purpose recurs and a new loan is needed.
- **Rule of 78s**—The most common method of calculating the rebate of prepaid interest charges on an installment loan when the loan is paid off before its scheduled maturity.
- **Security**—A tangible asset that a borrower pledges to a lender in order to obtain a loan. If the borrower defaults, the security may be sold by the lender to satisfy the debt.
- **Simple interest**—One means of calculating loan costs, usually in a loan payable in one lump as opposed to installments. The interest cost is expressed as a percent of the amount borrowed, usually on an annual basis. Example: 10 percent annual simple interest on a $1,000 loan would be $100 for a 1-year loan, $50 for a 6-month loan, and $25 for a 3-month loan.

Self-Test

1. The "Morris Plan" is the origin of the installment payment plan.
  a. true
  b. false

2. If you do not want unfavorable credit information made public, a credit bureau will remove it from your file for a nominal fee.
  a. true
  b. false

3. If you obtain a "prime rate" loan, you have probably secured the lowest interest rate available at that financial institution.
  a. true
  b. false

4. Most installment loans are written as variable-rate contracts.
  a. true
  b. false

5. The purpose of a cosigner is to provide the lender with the name of a person who can verify the borrower's credit repayment ability and character.
  a. true
  b. false

6. Pyramiding is a credit abuse that occurs when a loan for a recurring purpose is not paid off by the time that purpose recurs.
   a. true
   b. false
7. Under the Rule of 78s, a borrower who pays off a 12-month installment loan at the end of the eighth month is entitled to a rebate of 25 percent of the original cost of interest.
   a. true
   b. false
8. Which of the following terms refers to the amount of borrowing an individual can realistically handle with their current and anticipated income and expenses?
   a. credit needs
   b. credit capacity
   c. credit history
   d. credit access
9. The annual dollar interest charge on a $1,000, 12-month installment loan, using a 12 percent add-on interest calculation, would be
   a. $12.
   b. $120.
   c. $93.33.
   d. $1,120.
10. Simple interest loans
    a. are available only to businesses.
    b. are usually associated with a very high rate of interest.
    c. are generally repayable in one lump at a specified time.
    d. both a and c.
11. Under federal law, interest rates on loans must be expressed to the borrower using
    a. simple interest rates.
    b. add-on interest rates.
    c. discount interest rates.
    d. annual percentage rates.
12. This form of credit abuse occurs when small monthly payments are charged for most of the term of a loan, with one large final payment.
    a. oversecuring
    b. pyramiding
    c. usury
    d. ballooning

Using What You've Learned

Title: Low-Down-Payment Long-Term Loans

Purpose: To familiarize you with the impact of the amount of down payment and duration of a loan on the cost of interest and monthly payments.

Description: You have decided to purchase a bedroom set costing a total of $3,000 and plan to make a $500 down payment, financing the balance over a 24-month period. The loan is financed at 12 percent add-on interest:

$3,000	purchase price
− 500	down payment
$2,500	amount to be financed
× .12	interest of 12%
300	interest for 1 year
× 2	
600	interest for 2 years
+ 2,500	amount to be financed
3,100	principal plus interest
÷ *24*	term of loan
$ 129.16	monthly payment

Assume you have an additional $1,000 available that you could apply toward the down payment and still maintain a comfortable "emergency fund."

Task:

Calculate the total interest and monthly payments, using the same 12 percent add-on interest but making the following substitutions:

$1,000 down payment; 24-month duration:

Interest: $ __________ Monthly payments: $ __________

$1,000 down payment; 18-month duration:

Interest: $ __________ Monthly payments: $ __________

$1,500 down payment; 24-month duration:

Interest: $ __________ Monthly payments: $ __________

$1,500 down payment; 18-month duration:

Interest: $ __________ Monthly payments: $ __________

Do the comparative monthly payments and total interest charges influence your decision about the size of the down payment you will make and the length of the loan? Which of the above options would you select and why? Did you discover another combination that is more advantageous?

____

____

____

____

If you had to withdraw the extra down payment money from a money fund account that has averaged 14 percent interest over the previous 12-month period instead of from a passbook savings account paying 5¼ percent, would your decision be different? Why?

____

____

____

____

PART FIVE

MAKING YOUR MONEY GROW

CHAPTER

15

Making Your Money Grow

Overview

An essential part of any financial program involves the investment of dollars for the future. Some of the ways dollars can be accumulated involve a high degree of risk; others are relatively safe. Some investments offer a comfortable measure of protection against inflation, while others grant little or none at all. Some ways seem simple, others seem complicated; some require luck, others prudence. The challenge is to find the program that will enable you to accumulate the future dollars you need safely, comfortably, and in a manner that does not interfere with your ability to pursue your current needs and desires.

One of the ways to make your money grow is to lend it to another person or institution with the understanding that they will pay interest for its use. This is referred to as **fixed income investing.** A savings account is a familiar example of this approach to accumulating dollars.

Another option is to buy something you believe will generate income and increase in value while you hold it. For example, if you buy part ownership in a company, you anticipate that the company will be profitable and that it will distribute a portion of its profits to its owners. You also hope that the company will prosper and that the value of your ownership interest will increase, allowing you to sell it at a profit in the future.

The distinction between lending money to reliable debtors and buying something with dollars is critical. When you lend, you have a binding legal contract that promises the return of your principal plus interest. When you buy, you are an owner and you have to take your chances that you can get your money back at any time you wish.

In examining various investment programs, you will soon discover that the larger the possible reward, the greater the risk. Put the other way around, the safer your money is, the less return you can expect. In planning a program of savings and investments (commonly known as a **portfolio**), consider the following criteria:

- **Liquidity.** Liquidity refers to how quickly and conveniently you can retrieve your money, and at what cost, if any. For example, with a regular savings account, you can claim all your money plus accrued interest immediately by simply requesting it. In contrast, liquidating a savings certificate before the end of the agreed-on term might result in forfeiture of a portion of the interest and principal. Generally, though, the certificate pays a higher rate of interest than a regular passbook savings account. The amount of liquidity you need, or can forgo, depends on the nature and timing of your individual needs.
- **Yield.** Generally, yield refers to how much money your savings or investments earn for you. The term "yield" is often used interchangeably with "return" or "return on investment." In making any form of investment, you should determine not only what yield you can expect immediately but whether

that yield will continue, for how long, and what degree of fluctuation it might be subject to.

- **Pledge value.** You may, from time to time, have an unexpected need for money. The pledge value of any investment is a measure of the percentage of the investment's value you can borrow, how quickly you can get the money, and how much it will cost you. Among the things you can pledge for a loan are:
  - savings accounts—passbook and certificate
  - stocks
  - good-quality real estate
- **Hedge value.** You should consider the ability of your investments to withstand the effects of inflation. This aspect of an investment is called its hedge value. Real estate has long been considered a good hedge against inflation, but the hedge value of a specific property depends on the nature of the property, the management of the property, and trends in the community in which it is located.

All investors, large and small, should pay constant attention to the tax implications of the various types of investments available. Tax implications divide investments into three broad categories: taxable, tax-deferred or tax-sheltered, and tax-exempt.

- **Taxable investments.** All money earned on a taxable investment is taxed the same year in which it is earned. Included in this category are such investments as savings accounts, corporate and government bonds, and dividens earned on stocks.
- **Tax-deferred or tax-sheltered investments.** The payment of taxes on income earned through these investments can be delayed until some future time. This decreases the cost of the investment and adds to its return. The best example of a tax-deferred investment is the Individual Retirement Account, or IRA. This investment allows you to invest money for retirement. The amount invested in the plan each year is a form of tax deduction, and the interest earned over the years is not subject to taxation, making it possible to shelter a portion of your income from taxation while building a retirement resource. The Tax Reform Act of 1986 cut deeply into the benefits from this type of investing. Many of the tax breaks available through shelter plans have been eliminated entirely.
- **Tax-exempt investments.** All or most of the income generated from this kind of investment is tax-free. If you buy a municipal bond, for example, and hold it to maturity, you pay no tax on the interest it earns for you. Investors should note, however, that some municipal bonds are now taxable as a result of the 1986 Tax Reform Act. A U.S. Supreme Court decision in April 1988 empowered Congress to tax interest earned on municipal bonds. This could go into effect in 1989 or later. But, if you sell the bond or bonds for profit, that profit is taxable income, even though any interest the bond earned before the sale is not taxable.

"Investigate before you invest" is an essential maxim to remember when putting your money to work. An equally important idea, which is too frequently ignored, is "investigate before you un-invest." The literature published every year on investments is vast. Although it's impossible to keep up with the outpouring of books, magazine and newspaper articles, reports and analyses, you may want to begin your investigation with the following:

- Books on the subject of basic money management and investment programs. One perennially reliable source is *Dun and Bradstreet's Guide to Your Investments.*

- Magazines: *Newsweek, U.S. News and World Report, Forbes, Financial World, Fortune, Business Week, Money, Changing Times,* and *Barron's.*
- Newspapers: *Wall Street Journal.*
- Seminars and courses, particularly the ones conducted by community colleges, universities, and financial firms.
- National Public Broadcasting System (PBS) and Cable Network News (CNN) offer a variety of television programs on money and investments.

Learning Objectives

When you complete this lesson, you should be able to:

- Show the relationship between the yield that can be expected from an investment and the amount of risk involved.
- Define and calculate the yield on an investment.
- Explain how pledge value can be an aid in obtaining a low-interest loan.
- Identify the particulars of the federal income tax laws concerning taxes on dividends and interest.
- Discuss the theory behind a tax-deferred investment.
- Recognize the appropriate time to invest in a tax-exempt municipal bond.
- List and describe sources for investment information.

Reading Assignment

Read Chapter 15 of the text, "Making Your Money Grow: An Overview," pages 340–355.

Key Terms and Phrases

- **Discretionary income**—Extra money available after one's basic needs have been paid for.
- **Hedge value**—Generally, the ability of an investment to withstand the effects of inflation.
- **Liquidity**—Generally, how quickly, conveniently, and cheaply you can retrieve your money from an investment.
- **Pledge value**—Generally, the ease and cost of borrowing against a particular investment.
- **Reward/Risk rule**—An investment adage that correctly states that the greater return you expect on an investment, the greater risk you'll be taking.
- **Tax-deferred (tax-sheltered) investments**—Investments whose earnings are not subject to taxation during the year earned but will be in some later year.
- **Tax-exempt investments**—Investments with earnings not subject to taxation at any time.
- **Taxable investments**—Investments with earnings subject to taxation in the year earned.
- **Yield**—Earnings you receive from an investment; generally expressed as a percentage. For example, a return of $5 in one year on an investment of $100 equals a yield of 5 percent.

Self-test

1. Usually, the riskier an investment is, the lower the yield will be.
   a. true
   b. false
2. Common stock generally has a more favorable pledge value than a savings account.
   a. true
   b. false
3. Generally, interest earned on savings accounts is subject to federal income taxes.
   a. true
   b. false
4. The interest earned on municipal bonds is exempt from federal income taxes.
   a. true
   b. false
5. Hedge value is usually associated with, and compared to, the rate of inflation.
   a. true
   b. false
6. The yield on common stocks remains the same from year to year.
   a. true
   b. false
7. The risk/reward rule is associated with
   a. safety.
   b. liquidity.
   c. pledge value.
   d. hedge value.
8. Which of the following refers to the speed with which money can be retrieved from an investment?
   a. safety factor
   b. yield factor
   c. hedge value factor
   d. liquidity factor
9. The extra money available after basic needs have been paid for is called
   a. inheritance.
   b. net pay.
   c. discretionary income.
   d. taxable income.
10. Income on stocks is referred to as
    a. interest
    b. dividends
    c. tax-sheltered income.
    d. discretionary income.
11. Which of the following generally has the best pledge value?
    a. stocks.
    b. passbook savings accounts
    c. bonds
    d. diamonds

Using What You've Learned

Title: Financial Publications Analysis

Purpose: To examine several financial publications for advice on the current and future state of the economy and for recommendations on how to invest your money.

Description: This project will familiarize you with obtaining from investment publications information that will assist you in making investment decisions.

Task: Decide on a particular date, and read selected articles from as many of the listed publications as possible, being sure all of them cover the same period of time. Record their predictions regarding the economy and their recommendations on a specific type of investment of your choosing (gold, airlines, steel industry, etc.). Answer the questions that follow.

Publication	Predictions Regarding the Economy	Investment Recommendations
Forbes		
Fortune		
Business Week		
Money		
Changing Times		
Wall Street Journal		
Any brokerage firm's advertisement letter		

Is there a consensus regarding the state of the economy?

____

____

____

What is the most frequently recommended investment? Why?

____

____

____

What is your opinion of these publications and their current advice?

____

____

____

CHAPTER

16

The Money Market

Overview

As discussed in Lesson 15, there are two basic ways of making your money grow. One is to lend it to others in return for a fee known as interest. The other way is to buy something (such as stock or real estate) and hope that you can sell it later for more than you paid. During the time you own the share or property, you may also receive a portion of the profits if, in fact, profits are generated.

The arena in which you find opportunities for lending is known as the **money market.** The money market is not a place but a concept. When you open a savings account or buy a U.S. Savings Bond, you have entered into a money market transaction: you have lent your money to a bank or to the government, and you have received their promise to repay you. In a more technical sense, the money market refers to certain transactions involving short-term government and corporation bonds.

Interest is the fee a borrower pays in order to have the use of someone else's money. Interest is normally expressed as a percentage of the total amount borrowed, calculated on a yearly basis. **Compounding** means that the interest you earn stays in your account and begins to earn interest itself.

Savings plans can differ with respect to the manner in which interest is actually credited to an account. Many institutions credit interest from the day a deposit is made until the day it is withdrawn. Some require that the money remain in the account for a full calendar quarter in order to earn interest. Others use the low balance in any quarter as the basis for computing the interest. Determining the true yield on a money market investment requires more than just examining the rate of interest being paid. You must examine the frequency of compounding and crediting of interest to the accounts as well.

The variety of money market investment opportunities is staggering by comparison to those available 20 years ago. As borrowers compete ever more aggressively for investors' dollars, new techniques and opportunities for money market investments are emerging at a rapid pace. Opportunities available to you include:

- **Passbook savings accounts.** A passbook savings account is an "open-end" agreement between a customer and a financial institution. The customer is free to deposit as much money as desired at any time. While the money is in the account, it will earn interest in accordance with the agreement set forth between the institution and the investor. The institution may reserve the right to alter the interest rate being paid after giving proper notice to its investors.
- **Money market accounts. Although money market accounts generally require a fairly high minimum deposit, they pay a higher rate of interest than passbook accounts and are just as flexible, allowing withdrawals at any time.**
- **Certificates of deposit.** Certificates of deposit, or CDs, are fixed contracts for a specific duration and amount of money, paying a fixed interest rate. The interest rate payable on any certificate depends on general interest rate conditions at the time the investment is made. Since certificates of deposit are firm

contracts for a set amount of time, you can expect to be penalized if you withdraw money from your certificate before the maturity date.

Government regulations have changed from time to time with respect to the amount of penalties that can be charged.

In recent years, deregulation has made it possible for institutions to offer a vast assortment of savings certificates. With such a myriad of choices available, making the right decision becomes a complex matter. A number of factors should be considered:

- Is the interest rate offered fixed or variable?
- How often is the interest compounded?
- Is a minimum deposit required?
- Are higher interest rates provided for larger investments? At what levels?
- Can you place additional sums of money into your certificate account? How will the interest be affected?
- Can you borrow against your certificate? How does the rate charged compare to the penalty for early withdrawal?

Examine each savings certificate investment in terms of its yield, liquidity, hedge value, safety, pledge value, and tax implications.

Just as individuals often borrow money to buy a car or make home improvements, businesses and governments also borrow money. They may borrow for a long term or short term, for a few years or a few months. When they borrow for a long term, the IOU they issue is referred to as a bond.

There are three major categories of bonds: federal government, local government, and corporate. And there are three different ways an investor can be involved in bonds: directly, semidirectly, and indirectly.

You can buy various bonds directly through a stockbroker and, in some cases, through the investment departments of major banks. You can invest in them semidirectly through the investment departments of major banks or mutual funds that pool the investments of many individuals and spread them out over a wide assortment of different issues. If you have a bank account, an insurance policy, or pension fund, it's very likely that some of your money is already invested in the bond market.

U.S. Savings Bonds are the most commonly known bonds issued by the federal government. They are currently called EE and HH bonds. EE bonds, sold since November 1, 1982, offer a fluctuating rate of interest. The interest on E or EE bonds is exempt from state and local taxes and is subject to federal income taxation only when the bonds are cashed. In contrast, the assured interest on HH bonds is taxable the year in which it is received.

Zero coupon bonds, a new type of investment, involve the purchase of bonds at one price and their redemption a set period of time later for a much higher price. Although zero coupon bonds do not pay interest as such, the IRS has ruled that potential earnings must be reported and taxed each year. For this reason, such investments may be most appropriate for IRA and Keogh plans.

Under the overall heading of **corporate bonds** are included the IOUs issued by railroads, public utilities, and industrial firms. Corporate bonds can usually be bought in denominations of $1,000, and the commission payable to a stockbroker is generally much less than for buying stock.

Corporate bonds are rated according to quality by two companies: Standard & Poor's and Moody's. The two ratings take into account the basic financial strength of a corporation and its ability to pay the interest on its debts. Highest-rated bonds offer the lowest rate of interest and lowest risk to investors. The ratings go from

AAA for the highest-grade obligations to DDD-D for bonds in default, where the rating indicates the relative salvage value.

Bonds had historically been considered a safe haven for investors' money. Many companies weren't able to raise funds by issuing IOUs because they weren't creditworthy enough—perhaps they had not been in business long enough or their financial affairs were not strong enough. But, among these companies, there had to be many that were perfectly honorable, reliable, creditworthy, and able to deliver interest and principal payments as promised. In the mid-1980s, a concept emerged that enabled many of these companies to borrow money in the bond market, albeit at higher rates of interest than their more creditworthy or experienced peers.

As a rule, these corporations were rated BBB or lower. Because of their lower ratings, these instruments became known as "junk bonds," even though many of them were of reasonably good quality. Depending on overall conditions in the economy, junk bonds pay roughly 3 to 5 percent more than U.S. Treasury Bonds. A careful analysis of any given junk bond or mutual fund portfolio of such bonds could turn up good bargains. Note that, in times of economic downturn or fluctuations, junk bonds are more likely to suffer a steeper drop than higher-rated bonds.

States, cities, towns, water districts, school districts, highway authorities, and a variety of other local entities also have the periodic need to borrow funds. As of 1988, we have tax-exempt and taxable mutual bonds. Further, a 1988 U.S. Supreme Court decision gave Congress the power to tax bonds that had previously been fully tax-exempt. The extent to which this power will be used is unknown. However, if you buy a municipal bond and later sell it at a profit, that profit is subject to full federal and state income taxes. Municipal bonds are rated by the same two services that rate corporate bonds. As with corporate bonds, these rating services examine the financial status of the municipalities and compare the relative qualities of the various issues.

Over the last decade, the ingenuity of the financial marketplace has been particularly bright with respect to the creation of new and unusual forms of fixed income investment. As the competition for investment dollars has heightened, the pool of potential investors has been enlarged to allow the small investor access to such investment opportunities as mutual funds, corporate bond funds, municipal funds, money market mutual funds, convertible bonds, commerical paper, and banker's acceptance.

Learning Objectives

When you complete this lesson, you should be able to:

- □ List and evaluate the various types of savings plans available from financial institutions.
- □ Explain why corporate bonds fluctuate in value.
- □ Describe the tax implications of investments in U.S. Savings Bonds: Series E, EE, H, and HH. (E and H bonds were sold prior to 1980.)
- □ Explain how zero coupon bonds operate and what tax implications they have for the investor.
- □ Discuss the purpose of a municipal bond issue and its tax implications.
- □ Define the term "mutual fund" and explain how it operates.
- □ Compare each of the money market investments discussed in this lesson on the basis of safety, liquidity, yield, hedge value, pledge value, and tax implications.

Reading Assignment

Read Chapter 16 of the text, "Making Your Money Grow: The Money Market," pages 356–387.

Key Terms and Phrases

- ☐ **Banker's acceptance**—A form of investment that arises when a bank holds a foreign company's promissory note (IOU) and sells portions of that note to investors.
- ☐ **Call privilege**—The right of a corporation or other issuer of debt to pay off the holders of the debt at an agreed-on price prior to the scheduled maturity of the debt.
- ☐ **Certificate of deposit**—A contractual investment with a financial institution wherein the investor agrees to deposit a fixed sum of money for a fixed amount of time in return for a guaranteed interest rate.
- ☐ **Closed-end mutual fund**—These funds function in much the same way as open-ended funds, but investors buy shares in such funds on the stock market rather than dealing directly with the mutual fund company.
- ☐ **Commercial paper**—An instrument of short-term debt issued by a corporation.
- ☐ **Compounding of interest**—Occurs when the interest you earn stays in your account and begins to earn interest itself.
- ☐ **Convertible bond**—A corporate bond that gives the owner the right to convert the bonds into common stock of the issuing company upon stated terms and conditions.
- ☐ **Corporate bond**—A long-term debt instrument issued by a corporation.
- ☐ **Federal Deposit Insurance Corporation (FDIC)**—The federal agency that insures accounts in commercial banks and mutual savings banks against the failure of the institution.
- ☐ **Floating-rate bond**—A bond in which the interest rate payable to holders fluctuates up and down, usually within set limits and/or in accordance with some outside index.
- ☐ **Federal Savings and Loan Insurance Corporation (FSLIC)**—The federal agency that insures accounts in savings and loan associations against the failure of the institutions.
- ☐ **General obligation bond**—A type of municipal bond backed by the taxing authority of the municipality.
- ☐ **Government bond mutual fund**—Funds that invest in U.S. government securities including bills, notes, bonds, federal agencies, and the government-backed mortgage pools.
- ☐ **Junk bonds**—Bonds issued by less "proven"—thus higher-risk—corporations. They pay a correspondingly higher rate of interest.
- ☐ **Load charge**—The sale commission investors pay at the time they invest in a mutual fund.
- ☐ **Money market instruments**—Generally, short-term, high-quality investments, including certificates of deposit, bonds, repurchase agreements, commercial paper, and banker's acceptance.
- ☐ **Money market funds**—Mutual funds that specialize in acquiring high-interest-rate money market instruments.

- □ **Municipal bond**—A debt issued by a local government agency (state, city, county, or subdivisions thereof). Interest earned by investors in some such bonds is exempt from federal income taxes.
- □ **Mutual fund**—A pooling of the money of many investors which, under professional management, attempts to fulfill stated investment objectives.
- □ **National Credit Union Administration (NCUA)**—The agency that insures accounts in federally covered credit unions.
- □ **Open-end mutual fund**—A mutual fund in which portfolio managers buy and sell securities as their judgment dictates.
- □ **Revenue bond**—A type of municipal bond backed by the revenues produced by the entity borrowing the money (a toll road, for instance).
- □ **Sinking fund**—A reserve account set up by a corporation; money is put into the account each year, to be used to pay off a debt of the corporation when it falls due.
- □ **Treasury Bill**—A short-term (less than one year) federal government debt instrument; minimum denomination $10,000. (Many financial institutions offer savings certificates with terms similar to those of Treasury Bills. Such certificates are frequently called "Treasury Bill certificates" or "money market certificates.")
- □ **Treasury Bond**—A long-term (up to 20 years, or more) federal debt instrument.
- □ **Treasury Note**—A medium-term (one to seven years) federal government debt instrument.
- □ **Zero coupon bonds**—Bonds that offer a guaranteed return for a set period of time. Most commonly traded zero coupon bonds are derived from U.S. Treasury issues.

Self-Test

1. The more frequently interest is compounded, the more interest is earned on a savings account.
a. true
b. false

2. All regular savings accounts in financial institutions are insured up to $100,000 by either the FDIC or FSLIC.
a. true
b. false

3. If a $1,000 corporate bond is listed in a bond quotation table at "95," it means that the bond is selling for $950.
a. true
b. false

4. If the highest grade of AAA is given to a corporate bond by Standard & Poor, it means the bond is paying the highest interest rate possible in the current interest market.
a. true
b. false

5. One of the primary differences between a Series HH and Series EE U.S. Savings Bond is that the former pays a fluctuating rate of interest.
a. true
b. false

6. Although zero coupon bonds do not pay interest as such, investors are still subject to yearly taxation on the level of earnings generated during the calendar year.

a. true
b. false

7. Interest earned on which of the following money market instruments is not subject to federal income taxes?
 a. U.S. Savings Bond
 b. municipal bond
 c. corporate bond
 d. small-saver certificate
8. Of the following instruments, which one usually requires a minimum investment of $10,000?
 a. Treasury Bill
 b. U.S. Savings Bond, Series HH
 c. corporate bond
 d. mutual bond
9. What redemption value does a 30-year, $1,000 corporate bond, 8 percent yield, issued in 1960, have in 1990?
 a. $1,000 plus 240 percent
 b. $2,400
 c. $1,000
 d. the redemption value depends on the interest rates in 1990.
10. Which type of investment offers the best safety factor?
 a. common stock
 b. corporate bond
 c. municipal bond
 d. U.S. Savings Bond
11. The coupon yield on corporate bonds
 a. can fluctuate from year to year.
 b. is fixed for the duration of the bond.
 c. will increase if the corporation makes more money.
 d. will increase if the rate on municipal bonds increases.
12. Which of the following investments cannot be pledged as security for a loan?
 a. U.S. Savings Bonds
 b. municipal bonds
 c. nonrevenue corporate bonds
 d. callable corporate bonds

Using What You've Learned

Title: Selecting an Appropriate Investment

Purpose: This project will provide you with experience in selecting an appropriate investment approach in a variety of situations.

Description: Evaluate each of the following situations, and decide which type of investment is the most advantageous, given the circumstances. Take into account the investment criteria discussed in Lesson 15.

Task: Evaluate the following situations, decide what investments are most appropriate, and state your rationale. Choose one or more of the following investment options:

- ☐ passbook savings account
- ☐ certificate of deposit
- ☐ zero coupon bonds
- ☐ corporate bonds
- ☐ municipal bonds
- ☐ money market mutual funds
- ☐ U.S. Savings Bonds

A recently divorced 28-year-old woman with two elementary school–age children has $5,000 invested in a passbook savings account. With careful planning and budgeting, she is able to meet basic living expenses each month on the money she earns. She receives sporadic child support from her ex-husband. She would like to make her savings work for her, but fears she might need to use at least a portion of it if her car needs major servicing or a medical emergency arises.

A 45-year-old doctor with his own practice makes enough money to support his family (wife and three teenage children), with discretionary funds to spare each month. The family has invested in a large home, but the tax write-offs that result from that purchase are not sufficient to lower his federal income tax obligation to any extent. His main concern is defraying taxes; investment income is a secondary interest.

A married couple, both 55 years of age, have recently seen the last of their children through college and find they can now live comfortably on the husband's income alone, in the home they have owned for 25 years. Both of them have pension plans through their jobs but are concerned about living on a fixed income when they retire and would like to make some income-producing investments.

CHAPTER

17

The Stock Market

Overview

The stock market involves aspects of risk not found in money market investments. The nature of those risks is not always clear to prospective investors and speculators. To help you understand these risks, this lesson deals with how a corporation works, how stocks are traded, how to select stocks and mutual funds, basic terms used in connection with the stock market, and choosing a broker.

A corporation is a legal entity in its own right. Each separate state has its own specific laws governing how a corporation may be created and funded. Like a person, a corporation can be taxed. It can sue and be sued, and it can conduct business.

A corporation is owned by stockholders. Operating within the framework of applicable laws, the stockholders determine what they wish their corporation to do. In large organizations, the stockholders elect a group of directors to act on their behalf in setting policy and direction for the corporation. In turn, the directors choose corporate officers to carry out the day-to-day operation of the business.

When a person buys stock in a corporation, that person becomes a part owner of the business. The new stockholder has no promise that he or she will receive any fee for the money invested or that anyone will be obligated to pay that money back. If the business grows, the value of the corporation goes up, as does the value of the share that stockholder has in the corporation. If profits are generated by the corporation, a portion of the profits may be distributed to the stockholders. This distribution is called a **dividend** and represents a second way a stock investor can make money on his or her investment.

Years ago, **stock exchanges** were created to provide a ready marketplace for both buyers and sellers of stock in corporations. The stock exchanges are a form of auction in which buyers and sellers try to achieve the best buying or selling price. An investor who wishes to buy or sell stock places an order with a local stockbroker who works for a firm who owns a "seat" on an exchange. Each stock traded on an exchange is represented by a specialist, whose job it is to match buy and sell orders. To do so, the specialist may be required actually to buy or sell stocks from his or her own account.

If you want to buy or sell stocks, you will probably call a broker and place an order for the desired transaction. There are a variety of orders you can give your broker: market orders, limit orders, time orders, or fill or kill orders. Your approach, and the kinds of stocks you choose to buy or sell are influenced by what motivates your investment.

Some stock investors are "out to make a fast buck," an approach involving speculative stocks and high risks that is closer to gambling than investing. A less speculative method is the long-term growth approach. The investor with this objective will invest in industries and specific companies whose long-term future looks healthy and profitable. An immediate advantage of this approach over short-term trading is that when a stock has been held for the minimum 12-month holding period, the profits from its sale are taxed at a long-term capital gains rate that is lower than for short-term gains. If the investor selects investments wisely, and has a little luck and a lot of patience, he or she is quite likely to achieve the desired objectives.

Stock market mutual funds pool the money of many small investors and place them in a broad portfolio of various stocks. There are hundreds of different mutual funds offering a wide variety of choices to the investor. The primary task of the investor is to determine whether the fund's objectives are in line with his or her own: short-term growth (performance funds), long-term growth, income, or a combination. These objectives are spelled out in the fund prospectus, which should be read before any investment decision is made.

The stock market, like other professions, has a language of its own. The "Key Terms and Phrases" section of this lesson will help the beginning stock investor understand the specialized language of the stock market.

It is important to choose a broker carefully, remembering that *you* must make the ultimate decision based on professional recommendations and advice. In choosing your stockbroker, consider these criteria: the match between the broker's investment philosophy and yours, his or her reputation for integrity and hard work (which you can sometimes learn from other customers), willingness to spend time helping you establish investment goals, and the amount of time devoted to achieving those objectives. Finally, your broker should inspire confidence in his or her work.

Learning Objectives

When you complete this lesson, you should be able to:

- □ Differentiate between a corporation stockholder and bondholder.
- □ Illustrate how stock is traded on a major stock exchange, describing in the process the major types of stock orders.
- □ Given a sample stock listing from a newspaper, explain what each symbol and figure indicates.
- □ List and discuss the purpose of three stock market averages.
- □ Differentiate between cash dividends, stock dividends, stock splitting, and stock options.
- □ Explain the difference between common stock and preferred stock, and identify the three major types of preferred stock.
- □ Differentiate between the value of a stock and the price of a stock.

Reading Assignment

Read Chapter 17 of the text, "Making Your Money Grow: The Stock Market," pages 388–429.

Key Terms and Phrases

- □ **Blue-chip stock**—Stocks of a company considered to have high investment quality: relatively stable prices and strong dividend payment history.
- □ **Buying long/selling short**—When an investor buys stock, hoping for an increase in value as well as receipt of dividends, he or she is buying long. This is

the most common type of stock transaction. Selling short enables an investor to profit from a declining stock.

- **Call option**—A contract that gives the owner the right to buy 100 shares of a given common stock at a predetermined price (the "strike price") at any time until a fixed future date.
- **Churning**—An improper practice wherein a stockbroker creates unnecessary and excessive trading in a customer's account to generate commissions.
- **Commissions**—Brokerage commissions are the fees received by brokerage firms for handling the buying and selling of stock.
- **Convertible preferred stock**—Preferred stock that may be converted into shares of the company's common stock at a preset ratio.
- **Cumulative preferred stock**—A preferred stock in which unpaid dividends accumulate and are paid back to shareholders in full before common stockholders can be paid any of their dividends.
- **Dividend**—That portion of a company's profit that the directors vote to pay out to stockholders; usually paid quarterly.
- **Dividend reinvestment plans**—Many companies offer an interesting alternative to the quarterly dividend checks usually paid to stockholders. They offer automatic reinvestment plans wherein dividends are used to purchase additional shares of stock in the company.
- **Dow Jones Industrial Average**—The most commonly referred to index of stock prices and their movements. It reflects the price of 30 major industrial stocks.
- **Ex-dividend date**—A date that determines whether a buyer of stock will be entitled to a recently declared dividend. One who buys before the ex-dividend date will receive the dividend; one who buys after that date will not.
- **Fill or kill order**—An order given to a stockbroker to buy or sell stocks at a specific price, with the understanding that if the order can't be filled immediately at the given price, the order will terminate.
- **Glamour stock**—Stock of a company that the investment community perceives as "hot," as a "winner." Compared to blue-chip stocks, glamour stocks are generally less stable in their prices and dividend payment records.
- **Growth stock**—A stock that has had a recent growth in value above and beyond the broad averages of stocks overall.
- **Income stock**—A stock that is expected to pay a high level of dividend income to holders.
- **Limit order**—An order given to a stockbroker to buy or sell stock within a high and/or low pice range.
- **Margin buying**—Buying stock partly with your own funds and partly with funds that you have borrowed from the stockbroker.
- **Market order**—An order given to a stockbroker to buy or sell stock at whatever the going price may be.
- **Odd lot**—A block of less than 100 shares of stock.
- **Preferred stock**—A class of stock wherein the owners of these shares have a higher claim to company dividends (and assets in the event of liquidation) than owners of common shares. Most preferred stock is cumulative, which means that unpaid dividends are accumulated and preferred shareholders must be paid in full on all back unpaid dividends before common stockholders can be paid any of their dividends. Dividends are usually paid quarterly.
- **Premium**—In option trading, the cost of purchasing a contract.
- **Price-earnings ratio (P–E ratio)**—The price of a given stock, divided by the per share earnings of the company. A low ratio tends to indicate a more conservative investment situation. A high ratio tends to indicate a more speculative situation.

- **Prospectus**—A document that corporations offering securities are required to publish, disclosing certain facts regarding the offering.
- **Proxy**—A write-in ballot used by stockholders of a corporation, which allows them to vote on the election of directors and other pertinent issues; used in place of personal attendance at stockholders' meetings.
- **Put option**—A contract that gives the holder the right to sell 100 shares of a given stock at a predetermined price by a given future date.
- **Round lot**—A block of 100 shares of stock or a block divisible by 100.
- **Securities and Exchange Commission (SEC)**—A federal regulatory agency that oversees the trading of stocks.
- **Securities Investors Protection Corporation (SIPC)**—A federal agency that insures certain aspects of investors' accounts with brokerage firms in the event of the firm's failure.
- **Short selling**—A speculative technique that, when successful, allows an investor to profit from the drop in value of shares of stock.
- **Strike price**—The price at which you can buy the underlying stock in a call option contract.
- **Time order**—An order to a stockbroker to buy or sell stock subject to a time deadline; usually attached to a limit order.
- **Warrant**—Sometimes part of a stock offering, it allows the holder to purchase shares of the company's stock at a set price for a limited period of time.

Self-Test

1. One of the advantages of a prospectus that has been filed with the Securities and Exchange Commission is that the investor can be assured that the federal government stands behind the quality of the stock being offered.
   a. true
   b. false
2. The dividend listed in the newspaper for a given stock refers to the dividends that are guaranteed to be paid by that company for the current year.
   a. true
   b. false
3. A stock split is generally viewed as an unfavorable sign since the price per share has been effectively lowered.
   a. true
   b. false
4. In general, trading in stock options is more sophisticated and more speculative than trading in common stocks.
   a. true
   b. false
5. The relative quality of common stocks, like bonds, is easily measured in terms of the degree of protection of principal and interest by such firms as Standard & Poor.
   a. true
   b. false
6. In essence, the value of a stock is the same as its current selling price.
   a. true
   b. false
7. A document published by a corporation containing specifics on the securities it intends to sell to the public is called a

a. prospectus.
b. proxy.
c. put option.
d. warrant to purchase.

8. This type of stock order instructs your stockholder to buy or sell shares of stock at whatever the going market price might be:
a. call order
b. limit order
c. market order
d. time order

9. Which of the following terms refers to stocks issued by major corporations with relatively stable stock prices and regular dividend payout histories?
a. income stock
b. growth stock
c. blue-chip stock
d. glamour stock

10. Which of the following terms describes a technique whereby you can sell stock you technically do not own but have borrowed from your stockbroker?
a. fill selling
b. selling long
c. selling short
d. time selling

11. This certificate entitles a stockholder to purchase a company's common stock at a fixed price for a specific period of time.
a. callable option
b. put option
c. time purchase
d. warrant

12. A company that pools the funds of a number of small investors and invests them in a broad portfolio of various securities is called
a. a board of directors.
b. a mutual fund.
c. the New York Stock Exchange.
d. the Securities and Exchange Commission.

Using What You've Learned

Title: What Stock to Buy

Purpose: This project describes several stock investment opportunities. You are asked to analyze each offering and make a decision as to its purchase. By doing this exercise, you will develop an appreciation for the information required to make a prudent stock purchase.

Description: You are asked to analyze several stock offerings. Some of the companies listed are actual stocks. Fill in the current market price and dividends, and evaluate these based on present circumstances. Others are fictional. Evaluate these based on what you know about the current marketplace.

Task: Complete the table that follows. Based on this information, decide whether to purchase each of the stocks listed. The first stock is given as an example.

	Potential for					
Description of Stock	Ongoing Dividend Income	Capital Growth Income	Security Factor	Purchase Advantages	Purchase Disadvantages	Purchase Decision and Rationale
EXAMPLE: International Business Machines Common Stock $110.00/share 4.4% dividend paid last year	Steady growth in dividends through the years. Trend likely to continue.	Good history of capital growth of stock value. Likely to continue.	Secure company. Not likely to go out of business.	Average dividend yield of 5% Excellent growth record: sales and income Leader in office machines and computers outlook for personal computers market continues to be good	Dividend is not outstanding. Increased competition from other companies in computer and office machine field.	Would buy stock for growth in value of shares. Home computer sales have good possibilities. Word processing equipment sales look good. The leader in the computer industry.
General Motors Common Stock $____/share, ____% dividend Listed on N.Y. Stock Exchange						

Description of Stock	Potential for: Ongoing Dividend Income	Potential for: Capital Growth Income	Security Factor	Purchase Advantages	Purchase Disadvantages	Purchase Decision and Rationale
Automated Data Processing $____/share, ____% dividend (This company is engaged in providing computer services to business firms.) Listed on N.Y. Stock Exchange						
Exxon Common Stock $____/share, ____% dividend Listed on N.Y. Stock Exchange						

Description of Stock	Potential for: Ongoing Dividend Income	Potential for: Capital Growth Income	Security Factor	Purchase Advantages	Purchase Disadvantages	Purchase Decision and Rationale
Caesar's (gambling and hotels) Common Stock $____/share, ____% dividend Listed on N.Y. Stock Exchange						
Eastern Airlines Common Stock $____/share, ____% dividend Listed on N.Y. Stock Exchange						

Description of Stock	Potential for: Ongoing Dividend Income	Potential for: Capital Growth Income	Security Factor	Purchase Advantages	Purchase Disadvantages	Purchase Decision and Rationale
Electric City Car Inc. Common Stock (Company established in 1982 to develop an electric car for city driving. Maximum speed: 30 MPH. One test model produced to date.) $3.00/share Not yet listed on any stock exchange.						

Description of Stock	Potential for Ongoing Dividend Income	Potential for Capital Growth Income	Security Factor	Purchase Advantages	Purchase Disadvantages	Purchase Decision and Rationale
Re-Cyk Garbage Co. Common Stock (New company seeking funds to develop equipment to process garbage into fuel and other products.) $5.00/share Not listed on any stock exchange.						

Description of Stock	Potential for Ongoing Dividend Income	Potential for Capital Growth Income	Security Factor	Purchase Advantages	Purchase Disadvantages	Purchase Decision and Rationale
ABM Computer Co. Common Stock (New company seeking funds to produce computers to compete with IBM. Several of founders are former IBM technicians.) $1.00/share offering price Not yet listed on any stock exchange.						

Description of Stock	Potential for: Ongoing Dividend Income	Potential for: Capital Growth Income	Security Factor	Purchase Advantages	Purchase Disadvantages	Purchase Decision and Rationale
McBurger Fast Food Sausages Common Stock (New company being formed to open fast food restaurants selling hot and sweet sausage sandwiches. Plans to open restaurants next to every McDonalds & Burger King.) $.25/share offering price, 0% dividend paid last year Not listed on any stock exchange.						

CHAPTER

18

Real Estate Investments

Overview

Real estate has a certain allure not found in other types of investing. The only tangible evidence of most investments is a piece of paper—a stock certificate, a savings document, a bond. But with real estate you own all or part of something that is real, something that you can live in, walk on, cultivate, and point to with pride. And therein may lie a serious flaw. Personal feelings and careful investment decisions don't always go hand in hand.

While there are a number of pitfalls associated with real estate investments, they can provide an attractive investment vehicle for the individual who is prepared to do the necessary homework. If the local market is properly researched, if the premises and legal documents are properly scrutinized, and if the required amount of time and patience are devoted to the project, real estate can be a productive long-term investment. The basic types of real estate investments are:

- **Income-producing real estate.** A building is purchased with the intent of renting it to generate income. At some future date, the sale of the building may produce a profit as well.
- **Vacant land investing.** The acquisition of unimproved land for purposes of renting it or selling it at some future date at a profit.
- **Turnover investing.** Property is purchased with the intent of reselling it as soon as possible at a profit. Income from renting the property is a secondary consideration.
- **Mortgage investing.** Money is lent to another, using real estate to secure the loan. No actual ownership interest in the property is acquired at the time of investment but could be if the borrower defaults, making knowledge of the value of the collateral real estate essential.
- **Group ventures.** A number of investors pool their money to invest in any or all of the above categories. Group ventures can include real estate investments, trusts, syndications, and partnerships.

The primary objective in investing in **income-producing real estate** is to earn income on your investment. A secondary objective is to obtain tax sheltering of that income through the depreciation deduction. Of course, there are many factors that can affect the amount of income the property will produce. In commercial properties, a broad spectrum of possible tenants could occupy any given space. This spectrum is limited only by the landlord's willingness to accept certain kinds of tenants and by zoning ordinances that might control the usage permitted in certain areas. When entering into a business venture, such as a lease, the landlord can and should check with the local credit bureau to determine the tenant's credit history.

The potential risks and rewards for the landlord are directly related to the quality, location, and nature of the building itself. As in buying a house, the would-be investor in income-producing real estate must pay explicit attention to the various mechanical and structural details of the building. An investor unfamiliar with building construction is wise to hire a construction specialist to provide a detailed inspection and report on the building.

Location is also an important consideration. For commercial property, one must determine whether traffic patterns or changes in adjoining neighborhoods can affect the investment. The nature of the building is also important. Many buildings are limited in use by their size, shape, and type of construction. The more limited the use of a building, the more difficult it may be to find tenants and maintain the level of return desired.

The job of managing rental property includes leasing the premises, collecting rent, supervising repairs, maintaining good public relations, and taking steps to improve the investment. A skilled property manager can be a very valuable ally for the real estate investor. In addition to attending to day-to-day operations, the manager is in close touch with the general real estate market within the community and might be able to spot potential tenants or buyers. A manager's familiarity with the property enables him or her to detect the need for preventive maintenance, which can preclude serious repairs and major replacement costs. The manager also absorbs many of the headaches inherent in real estate ownership.

The mechanics of financing income property are generally the same as financing personal property. The investor, unless paying cash, makes a down payment and either assumes an existing mortgage or obtains a mortgage loan from outside sources.

The astute investor will seek a good return on invested capital (the cash down payment) by structuring the mortgage so that adequate cash flow is available. In simple terms, the way to make money on residential or commercial property is to receive more in rents than is paid out in expenses. The difference is the return on your investment. As you might expect, taxes and depreciation are complicating factors.

Investing in **vacant** or **raw land** can be one of the most extreme forms of speculation. It remains, for the most part, the province of the skilled professional, who has the expertise, the capital, and the selling skills needed to turn a profit most of the time. Raw land investments require continual expenditures—real estate taxes, public liability insurance, security—while capital remains beyond reach until the land is sold. Even borrowing against raw land is extremely difficult.

Purchasing homes for subsequent resale is less speculative than raw land investments but more speculative than investing in higher-quality income property. **Turnover investing** involves seeking out houses that have god underlying value but can be bought for less than the normal market price. Profitable turnover investing involves the same considerations as buying a home: Can you afford to refurbish or repair the home to increase its value? Can you make the house more attractive by offering it as fully financed?

Technically, mortgages are not actually real estate investments, but many people think of them as such. **Mortgage investments** fall more aptly into the fixed income category. The investor is really buying someone else's IOU, with real estate as security. Because the investor owns the property if the borrower defaults, it is considered a real estate investment. The careful investor scrutinizes the value of the property itself, as well as the creditworthiness of the borrower. The same precautions a bank would exercise in making an original mortgage loan are necessary: appraising the property, determining the credit status of the borrower, and assuring adequate title and property insurance protection.

Instead of investing in a single mortgage, it is also possible to pool your money with other investors and purchase a share of a packaged assortment of mortgages. The most popular program for this type of investing is offered through the Government National Mortgage Association, an agency of the U.S. government. As a GNMA (or "Ginnie Mae") investor, you receive monthly checks just as if you owned a single mortgage.

Learning Objectives

When you complete this lesson, you should be able to:

- □ Distinguish between some myths and facts about real estate investing.
- □ Identify and discuss at least four factors that should be considered when investing in income-producing property.
- □ List and explain the important elements that should be part of a lease.
- □ Discuss the role of the depreciation deduction in income-producing real estate investments.
- □ Make a checklist of the items that should be considered when investing in vacant land.
- □ Explain the importance of obtaining an appraisal and survey before investing in raw land.
- □ List and describe the various types of mortgage investments, including mortgage pools.
- □ List the advantages of a real estate investment trust (REIT).

Reading Assignment

Read Chapter 18 of the text, "Making Your Money Grow: Real Estate and Other Opportunities", pages 430–453.

Key Terms and Phrases

- □ **Gross lease**—A commercial lease that requires the landlord to pay for virtually all expenses related to the property.
- □ **Group venture**—The pooling of money with several investors to purchase real estate (or other investments).
- □ **Income-producing property**—Generally, real estate purchased as an investment, from which rental income and depreciation deductions flow to the investor.
- □ **Mortgage investing**—A form of investment wherein someone else's IOU is purchased, using real estate as the security for the loan.
- □ —Mortgage pool—Investment programs that package a number of mortgages into a pool and offer a share of ownership to investors in the form of a certificate.
- □ **Net lease**—A type of commercial lease in which the tenant is responsible for most, or all, of the operating costs of the property.
- □ **Percentage clause**—A provision in a commercial lease that states, generally, that the tenant must pay the landlord a certain percentage of the tenant's dollar volume of business under agreed-on conditions.
- □ **Real estate investment trust (REIT)**—A form of mutual fund for real estate investors.
- □ **Take-back mortgage**—A situation in which the seller of property accepts the buyer's IOU instead of cash. The IOU is secured by a mortgage on the property.

- **Turnover investing**—With reference to real estate investing, a program of buying property with the intent to resell it at a profit as soon as possible.
- **Raw land investing**—A type of real estate innvestment involving the purchase of raw, or vacant, land for eventual personal use or subsequent resale, with the possibility of rental income in the interim.

Self-Test

1. Investing in real estate is very much like investing in the stock market: it offers an assured return on your money.
a. true
b. false

2. A gross lease requires the landlord to be responsible for all operating expenses on the rental property, including taxes, utilities, maintenance, and cleaning.
a. true
b. false

3. One of the most attractive aspects of an income-producing real estate investment is the tax deduction allowed for the physical depreciation of a building.
a. true
b. false

4. One of the major advantages of investing in vacant land is that the land, providing it remains vacant, is not subject to local property taxes.
a. true
b. false

5. One of the advantages of a real estate investment trust (REIT) is that the investor need not be concerned with the daily management of the investment.
a. true
b. false

6. When a landlord requires a rental deposit, the tenant's obligation for any breakage or damage to the rental premises is limited to the amount of the deposit.
a. true
b. false

7. Purchasing a building and renting it out to tenants is a category of real estate investment known as
a. an income-producing investment.
b. investing in raw land.
c. mortgage investing.
d. turnover investing.

8. Which of the following is considered the most speculative category of real estate investing?
a. apartment building investments
b. income-producing investments
c. single-family house investments
d. raw land investments

9. When you sell property and agree to accept the buyer's IOU as full or partial payment, you have
a. arranged a mortgage overflow.
b. made a multimortgage arrangement.

c. exercised a seller's mortgage option.
d. taken back a mortgage.

10. Which of the following functions like a mutual fund, pooling the money of a number of investors to acquire real estate?
a. common stock fund
b. mortgage pool
c. real estate investment trust
d. small investors mutual fund

11. Which of the following represents a category of real estate investing in which money is lent to others, using real estate to secur the loan?
a. gross investing
b. mortgage investing
c. take back mortgage investing
d. turnover investing

Using What You've Learned

Title: What to Do with $80,000

Purpose: A hypothetical situation allows you to compare various investment alternatives, including maintaining an income property investment as well as other fixed investment options.

Description: Arthur Chudd has just inherited a $95,000 duplex that had been owned by his parents prior to their death in an automobile accident. After consultation with his tax accountant, he was advised that if he were to sell the duplex, he would have to pay a capital gains tax of $10,000 and a real estate commission of $5,000, leaving him with a balance of $80,000. He was also informed that if he rented both units, he would net a profit of $800 per month. The tenants would pay all utilities and property taxes.

Task: Arthur is very confused right now but must decide whether to sell the duplex or rent it out. He has asked for your advice. Complete the table that follows.

Item	Advice
If he sells the duplex, Arthur will have $80,000 to invest. Assuming he makes a conservative fixed investment (savings account, certificate of deposit, or bonds) how much can he expect to earn on his $8,000 (taxable investments/tax-exempt investments?)	
If he rents the units at the $800 monthly income rate, how much will he receive in yearly income?	
If he rents the duplex, what potential depreciation deduction can he expect? To what extent would his level of income affect the importance of this deduction?	

Item	Advice
Considering the current market, is there a possibility that the duplex would appreciate in value? Are rental units in demand in your area?	
What advice can you offer him regarding the lease if he decides to rent? What clauses should be included?	
If you were in Arthur's situation, what would you do? Support your financial decision.	

CHAPTER

19

Other Investment Opportunities

Overview

Beyond the money market, the stock market, and the real estate market, a whole galaxy of investment opportunities exists for making your money grow—or shrink. Some are offshoots of hobbies, such as collecting coins, stamps, beer cans, autographs, or commemorative medallions. Others are of a much more serious nature, such as commodities, equipment leasing, or investing in a business or franchise. The range of possibilities and risks is infinite.

Investing in an Existing Business

When a business is being sold or opened up to outside investors, the circumstances that motivate the owner's decision could be of vital importance to the investor. The owner may be seeking fresh capital for expansion, renovation, or new equipment. He or she might prefer to seek private financing rather than bank financing to save on interest, or for the flexibility of offering a share of the profits to an investor rather than paying interest on the loan.

With the aid of an accountant, the potential buyer should examine at least three years of operating statements and both state and federal tax returns. The flow of income and expenses should be traced to reveal trends that could indicate potential success or danger. Credit reports on the business and the principal owners will disclose whether obligations have been met. The possibility of new or threatening business competition should be investigated. The owner may be selling because plans for a major shopping center pose a serious competition problem.

If existing employees or the owner will be replaced in the day-to-day operation of the business, the extent of the business's success (or lack of it) that is due to their presence must be determined. Does the owner, for example, have a large loyal following that may disappear if he is no longer there?

An attorney should review the lease on the premises to determine how well protected the investor is. With the aid of an attorney, the parties will enter into a contractual agreement that spells out the rights and obligations of the parties, particularly regarding the ongoing management of the business. The contract will stipulate how profits are to be divided and losses covered. The contract will also protect the investor if it is later determined that the seller or borrower misrepresented the business.

Investing in a New Business

It's one thing to become involved in an existing business where there is a record of success and established customers. It's quite another to start a new business. Independently or through such means as a franchise agreement, it's pure speculation. Investors must proceed with a thorough understanding of the risks involved, realizing that the salesperson for a franchise is trying to assure his or her own profit in the venture. There is no assurance that the investor will realize a profit, or even see the original investment again.

Gambling in Commodities

Like raw land and new business ventures, the commodities market represents a form of speculation. In the commodities, or futures market, the investor is betting on the future prices of a variety of crops, metals, and international currencies. The chances of any bet succeeding are based not only on how others are betting but also on such totally unpredictable and uncontrollable factors as weather conditions, crop blights, the law of supply and demand, governmental and international politics, shifts in the world economy, and even consumer boycotts. Suffice it to say, investing in commodities is very risky, even for the most experienced investors. Anyone interested in learning about speculating in the commodity markets can obtain abundant information through a stockbroker or the respective exchanges.

Metals

Investments in precious metals such as gold, silver and, to an extent, platinum are also extremely risky, as evidenced in the early 1980s when the price of gold soared to over $825 an ounce. By late 1981, gold had plummeted to under $400 per ounce; a loss of more than 50 percent for those who bought at its peak, and many did. The gold roller coaster continued into early 1983 before it became relatively stable. Widespread abuses and fraudulent dealings frightened many prospective investors.

As with precious metals, strategic metals are often touted by promotors as an easy path to getting rich quick. Strategic metals are those that, at any given point in time, are considered important to national defense and industrial production but must be imported from other countries in large quantities. Advances in technology can render yesterday's boom tomorrow's disaster. Speculators who have the good luck to get in and get out at the right times might make some fast money. For the beginner, an investment in strategic metals is no place to build a solid foundation for future income.

Gemstones

The most popular form of gemstone speculation has traditionally been in diamonds, partially because they are easily appraised. But speculation in colored gemstones—rubies, emeralds, and sapphires primarily—has become popular as well. These opportunities are not restricted to big-money investors. Many plans are devised to appeal to small and medium-sized investors. And many of these plans are rife with danger.

One of the chief difficulties is that gemstones are as unique as snowflakes. Of a thousand diamonds, rubies, or sapphires examined, it's doubtful that two would be alike. To buy a gemstone without first having it independently appraised by a reputable jeweler or gemologist is extremely hazardous.

Collectibles

Anything that people like to collect and will buy to add to their collections is a collectible. The possibilities are limitless, ranging from old comic books to Chinese jade, from antique buttons to hubcaps, and everything in between. Whether purchased with due caution and deliberation as investments or bought in a mood of wild speculation, collectibles offer personal satisfaction to many. Nonetheless, it's wise to research both the objects themselves and markets for eventual resale before buying.

Whether you're investing in the money market or the stock market, gemstones or strategic metals, the best investment of all is an investment in knowledge. The world of money is changing at an increasingly rapid pace, and individual circumstances are changing with it. Taxes, interest rates, and government regulations all are in a state of flux. The investor cannot afford to ignore this outpouring of new information.

Learning Objectives

When you complete this lesson, you should be able to:

- □ List those factors that should be considered when investing in a small business.
- □ Explain why investing in commodities is a form of gambling.
- □ Outline the procedure for speculating in the currency of another country.
- □ Compare the advantages and disadvantages of speculating in gold or silver; in strategic metals.
- □ List those factors that should be considered when investing in gemstones.

Reading Assignment

Read Chapter 18 of the text, "Making Your Money Grow: Real Estate and Other Opportunities," pages 453–471.

Key Terms and Phrases

- □ **Commodities**—A variety of products (such as cattle, wheat, precious metals) whose future values are subject to fluctuation. Commodity markets offer the opportunity to speculate in those future values (also known as "future trading).
- □ **Foreign exchange**—Generally, the currency of other nations. The future values of the currencies of major nations can be bought and sold at commodity exchanges.
- □ **Strategic metals**—Metals that are considered important to our national defense and industrial production but that must be imported.

Self-Test

1. Starting a new business does not fall into any investment category and should be considered pure speculation.
  a. true
  b. false

2. Like raw land, the commodities market represents a form of pure speculation.
  a. true
  b. false

3. Commodity funds are somewhat less risky than direct speculation in commodities because of their diversification.
  a. true
  b. false

4. The foreign exchange market is considered less speculative than the commodities market.
  a. true
  b. false

5. One of the major advantages of buying gold or silver is that the investor is not likely to encounter fraud in the marketplace. The trading in these metals is totally regulated by the federal government.

a. true
b. false

6. Colored gemstones are more difficult to appraise than diamonds because of the wider range of color and chemical composition.
   a. true
   b. false
7. Of the following alternatives, which is generally the most speculative?
   a. buying an apartment building
   b. investing in an existing business
   c. buying a house in need of repair at a bargain price to resell
   d. starting a new business
8. Which of the following permits the investor to purchase an asset to be delivered in the future at a price agreed on at the time of the contract?
   a. asset delivery
   b. commodity contract
   c. franchise
   d. stock exchange
9. Metals considered important to national defense and industrial production are called
   a. precious metals.
   b. gemstones.
   c. gold and silver.
   d. strategic metals.

Using What You've Learned

Title: The Silver Glitter

Purpose: By investigating the various ways to acquire silver, you will become acquainted with the procedures for purchasing, the commission structures, price determinations and fluctuations, and the advantages and disadvantages of purchasing each of the different forms of silver.

Description This project will involve visiting a coin dealer to obtain information on purchasing silver. In each category given in the table, a number of options are available. For example, various sizes or weights of ingots and bars are available. You may want to specify circulated or uncirculated silver dollars or limit your choices by specifying coins minted in a certain year or at a particular mint. Discuss these choices with the coin dealer.

Task: Complete the following table with the information you gather, then make a purchase decision.

Form of Silver	Price Fluctuations last 12 months	Buying/Selling Commission	Ease of Buying/ Selling in the Open Market	How Is Price Determined	Dealer's Recommendation
Ingots					
Bars					
Junk silver coins					
Silver dollars					
Collectible coins					

Assume that you have $10,000 to gamble in the silver market. Based on your interview and the information from the table, what form(s) of silver would you buy? Explain your rationale.

____

____

____

____

____

PART SIX

PROTECTING WHAT YOU WORK FOR

CHAPTER

20

Life Insurance

Overview

Life is full of risks that cannot be adequately anticipated or prepared for. Some of these risks are conscious decisions: driving a car, taking on a new job, investing your money. Others, such as illness or natural disaster, may be strictly a matter of fate. You can take steps to minimize the impact of such events. Life insurance is one way to provide this kind of protection.

Life insurance is generally acquired in one of three ways: group plans, private plans, and credit plans.

- **Group plans.** Group life insurance is designed for large groups of people in similar circumstances. Your employer, for example, may provide a group life insurance plan for all employees who meet the necessary requirements of tenure on the job.
- **Private plans.** Private insurance is a direct contract between an individual and an insurance company.
- **Credit plans.** Credit insurance will pay the balance due on a loan if the borrower dies before it is paid off.

Types of Life Insurance Two basic types of life insurance are available: permanent and temporary or term. **Permanent insurance** is a lifetime contract. You agree to pay a fixed-level premium, and the insurance company agrees to deliver a stated sum of money at your death or, in certain cases, at an earlier time. In addition to the benefits payable on the death of the insured, the permanent policy builds up a "cash value," also referred to as a "nonforfeiture value." This permits the insured to terminate the policy and obtain either cash or some form of insurance, if desired, at some future time.

Term insurance is "pure" insurance. You obtain a fixed amount of protection at a fixed annual price for a limited amount of time. In general, term policies do not build the cash or nonforfeiture values found in permanent policies.

The initial out-of-pocket premium expense of term insurance is less costly than permanent life insurance. However, because term insurance is renewed at ever-increasing ages, and therefore increasing rates, the ultimate out-of-pocket expense can equal or exceed that of permanent life insurance.

Universal life insurance is a relative newcomer to the field; a variation of permanent or whole life insurance. In general, the universal policy allows the owner to make adjustments in the amount of coverage and the amount of premium to be paid, mixing investment features with insurance features. If the investment side of the contract does not perform well, there can be negative implications for the insurance side. For the relatively unsophisticated individual, the complexities and variabilities of universal life may render it not the best product for your needs.

As many as five parties can be involved in an insurance policy contract: the owner of the policy, the person whose life is insured, the beneficiary, the contingent beneficiary, and the insurance company. The policy itself is a legal contract that consists of a number of clauses.

- **The application.** The questionnaire the applicant must complete before the policy is issued is considered an important part of the policy.

- **Face value.** This is the amount of money due the beneficiary on the death of the insured.
- **Double indemnity.** This refers to the payment of double the face value of the policy in the event of accidental death as opposed to natural death—a clause available for an additional premium.
- **Incontestable clause.** Commonly, the insurance company will have a set period of time, usually two years, during which the company must take issue with any suspected false or misleading information contained in the application. During that initial period, a company can void the policy if improper statements were made.
- **Premium payments.** The policy contract will spell out the amount of the premium and how payments can be made: annually, semiannually, quarterly, or monthly.
- **Lapse, grace period, and reinstatement.** If a policyholder does not meet premium obligations, the policy lapses or is terminated. The policyholder has a grace period, usually of 31 days after the stated due date, during which he or she can still make a premium payment and continue the policy without penalty. Even after a policy has lapsed, the policyholder has a limited time to exercise his or her rights to reinstate it.
- **Waiver of premium.** This protection, usually available at a slight additional cost, provides that if the insured is totally disabled, the need to make premium payments will be waived.
- **Dividend options.** Some types of life insurance policies pay dividends to policyholders. If you own such a policy, you'll probably have a choice as to the manner in which those dividends are paid—in cash, applied toward the next premium due, used to purchase additional life insurance, and so forth.
- **Settlement options.** Policyholders may also have options concerning the manner in which the payment of proceeds will be made: in a lump sum or spread out over a period of time.
- **Conversion values.** Conversion (or nonforfeiture) values available to policyholders under permanent life insurance build up at various rates as premiums are paid over the years. Nonforfeiture values are based on the age of the insured at the time the policy is initiated.

Buying Life Insurance

Who needs life insurance? If you want to protect or enhance the financial welfare of anyone who is dependent on you, and your existing assets aren't adequate to provide the desired level of protection, you need life insurance. The first task in evaluating how much insurance is needed is to determine who is going to be protected by the program and to what extent. These are the goals you must define in order to reach dollar figures.

In choosing an insurance agent, as with any professional adviser, you must trust the agent's ability and have confidence in his or her training and integrity. Personal familiarity, recommendations from others, and reputation in the community are indicators. You might want to ask about the agent's credentials, background and training, and prior experience. Find out if the agent represents one company or the products of a number of different companies.

Learning Objectives

When you complete this lesson, you should be able to:

- State the main purpose of life insurance.
- Differentiate between a participating and nonparticipating life insurance policy;

between permanent and term life insurance; between variable and fixed annuities.

- □ List the advantages and disadvantages of group life insurance; of term life insurance.
- □ Explain the role of the beneficiary and contingent beneficiary in a life insurance policy.
- □ List and explain the various conversion values for a life insurance policy.
- □ Discuss those factors that should be considered when determining the amount of life insurance to purchase.

Reading Assignment

Read Chapter 19 of the text, "Life, Health, and Income Insurance," pages 474–499.

Key Terms and Phrases

- □ **Annuity**—A type of investment with an insurance company that guarantees the investor a fixed monthly income for a specific period of time.
- □ **Beneficiary**—One who receives the proceeds of a life insurance policy on the death of the insured person.
- □ **Benefits**—Money received from an insurance company when the insured party suffers a loss covered by the insurance policy.
- □ **Contingent beneficiary**—One who takes the place of an original beneficiary in an insurance policy, if the original beneficiary dies before the insured.
- □ **Decreasing term insurance**—A type of life insurance; the amount of coverage decreases from year to year.
- □ **Double indemnity**—A life insurance policy provision that will pay beneficiaries double the face value of the policy in the event of the accidental death of the insured.
- □ **Face value (amount)**—The amount of money a life insurance policy will pay to the beneficiary on the death of the insured.
- □ **Incontestable clause**—A provision in an insurance policy that cuts off the rights of the insurance company to challenge statements made in the application after a stated period of time.
- □ **Insurance policy**—A contract made with an insurance company wherein the company agrees to pay money to the named parties if certain events occur, such as the death, illness, or disability of the insured party; or damage to the insured's property (home, car).
- □ **Nonparticipating policy**—A life insurance policy in which dividends are not paid to the policyholders.
- □ **Owner**—The person who has the power to exercise various options within an insurance policy, including naming and changing the beneficiary, transferring ownership, making loans against the policy, or cashing it in.
- □ **Participating policy**—An insurance policy wherein policyholders participate in annual distributions of excess income generated by the company. These distributions are commonly known as dividends.
- □ **Permanent insurance**—Life insurance in which the amount of the premium paid remains fixed for the life of the policy. Also known as ordinary, straight, or whole life insurance.
- □ **Premium**—In insurance, the fee paid for coverage provided.

- **Settlement options**—Various ways in which the proceeds of a life insurance policy can be paid out.
- **Term insurance**—Also known as temporary insurance, a form of life insurance wherein the premium cost increases as the age of the insured increases. Policies run for a set number of years, and premiums are increased on renewal of policies.
- **Universal life insurance**—A variation of permanent insurance that combines investment and insurance features. It allows the owner to make adjustments in the amount of coverage and the amount of the premiums to be paid.
- **Waiver of premium**—A clause in an insurance contract (usually life, health, or disability plans) stating that if the insured becomes disabled, the need to pay the premiums on the policy will be waived during the period of disability.

Self-Test

1. A common feature of all life insurance policies is the fact that the younger you are when you initiate a contract, the lower your annual costs will be.
a. true
b. false

2. Premiums on participating life insurance policies are generally lower than premiums on nonparticipating life insurance policies.
a. true
b. false

3. In a life insurance contract, the contingent beneficiary takes the place of the original beneficiary if the original beneficiary dies before the insured.
a. true
b. false

4. A waiver of premium clause in a life insurance contract means that if the insured becomes disabled, the policy will remain in force without premium payments.
a. true
b. false

5. A person who is insured under a permanent life insurance policy and who is also the owner of the policy may cash in the policy for its cash value.
a. true
b. false

6. Life insurance proceeds are not subject to federal income taxes.
a. true
b. false

7. The primary objective of a family's life insurance portfolio is
a. to provide the parents with extra income if the children die.
b. to provide for a comfortable retirement.
c. to replace the source of income in the event of a breadwinner's death.
d. to put money aside in the early years to help pay for the children's college education.

8. The kind of life insurance policy issued by a mutual company in which dividends are paid to policyholders is called a
a. permanent policy.
b. participating policy.
c. nonparticipating policy.
d. stock dividend policy.

9. This type of life insurance is offered by a lender when you borrow money. It is designed to pay off the balance on a loan if the borrower dies before the loan is retired.
   - **a.** credit life insurance
   - **b.** group life insurance
   - **c.** annuity life insurance
   - **d.** participating life insurance
10. This type of life insurance is classified as temporary insurance and is designed to exist for a specific period of time, such as one year, five years, or ten years.
    - **a.** annuity
    - **b.** permanent insurance
    - **c.** straight life insurance
    - **d.** term insurance
11. Which of the following may the owner of a permanent life insurance policy not do?
    - **a.** borrow against it
    - **b.** cash it in for its face value within five years of originating the policy
    - **c.** convert it to extended term insurance
    - **d.** convert it to paid-up insurance
12. The clause in a life insurance policy that specifies the various ways in which the proceeds of the policy are to be paid to the beneficiary is called the
    - **a.** conversion option clause.
    - **b.** dividend option clause.
    - **c.** nonforfeiture option clause.
    - **d.** settlement option clause.

Using What You've Learned

Title: Do You Have Enough Life Insurance?

Purpose: This project requires you to obtain information about a family's current life insurance (preferably your own), analyze it, and offer suggestions.

Description: Examine your own life insurance coverage or obtain information about the life insurance held by a family with young children.

Task: Based on the information obtained, answer the following questions.

Describe the life insurance policies that you or the family interviewed currently have.

Husband: ____

____

____

Wife: ____

____

____

Children ____________________

____

____

If the husband were to die, assuming he is the main breadwinner, how would the wife handle the proceeds from his life insurance?

____

____

____

____

How would the husband handle the proceeds from the wife's policy if she died?

____

____

____

____

What provisions have been made for the children in the event both the husband and wife die?

____

____

____

____

If you or they have life insurance on the children, what are the reasons?

____

____

____

____

Prepare an analysis of your insurance package or coverage of the family you interviewed. Do you feel the coverage is adequate? Should the package be modified? What advice can you offer?

____

____

____

____

CHAPTER

21

Health and Income Insurance

Overview

Health and income insurance protect you against the costly ravages of medical problems. Many people have some form of health insurance through group plans at work, and most have a sick pay program that provides income from time off work due to illness or accident. But do these programs provide adequate protection with today's high costs of health care?

Out of every $3 currently spent on private health care and health care insurance premiums, only about $1 is returned to the public in the form of health insurance benefits. The other $2 is paid out of pocket, in spite of the fact that close to 90 percent of the working population is covered by one or more health insurance plans. This tremendous gap exists for a variety of reasons. Many individuals are not covered by health insurance or are protected for minor and probable medical expenses but not for major medical problems. Others may think their health insurance provides better protection than it really does.

If you don't know how well your insurance needs are covered, find out and take appropriate corrective steps. Be sure to review and update your health insurance policy regularly to make sure your coverage is keeping up with rising medical costs. Read and understand the small print in your policy. The large print giveth, and the small print taketh away.

Basic hospital, surgical, and physician insurance cover three different areas of medical costs. Frequently, they are lumped together in one basic policy.

- **Hospital insurance.** Hospital insurance is designed to reimburse the insured for medical expenses: room and board, nursing, minor supplies, and perhaps x-rays, tests, and medications.
- **Surgical insurance.** Surgical insurance pays for surgeon's fees and related expenses such as anesthesia, operating room fees, and assistant surgeons. Surgical policies may also provide some coverage for postoperative care and follow-up surgery if needed.
- **Physician insurance.** Generally, physician insurance, or basic medical insurance, is designed to pay doctor bills for hospital visits, office visits, and house calls.

A **major medical** policy is designed to protect you against major, unexpected, and catastrophic medical expenses. The initial costs absorbed by the insured are referred to as the **deductible.** Once the deductible has been met, the typical major medical policy will pay 80 percent of all additional costs, and the insured will have to pay the other 20 percent. There may also be a ceiling, a top limit of total expenses that the policy will pay.

A number of provisions that affect your rights appear in health insurance policies. The more important of these provisions are pre-existing conditions; excluded conditions; renewability; grace period, lapse, and reinstatement; maternity benefits; dependents' coverage; and waiver of premium.

In addition to the basic forms of medical insurance, there are other modes of protection that may be available. One, the health maintenance organization (HMO), offers a fairly comprehensive package. Others, such as Worker's Compensation, offer only a limited level of coverage.

Health maintenance organizations are a form of prepaid medical care facility. Instead of paying premiums to an insurance company and being reimbursed if and when medical expenses occur, the HMO provides a broad range of medical services in return for a fixed payment each month. Generally, you use the doctors and facilities provided by the HMO rather than choosing your own.

If you are injured at work, or if you contract an illness related to your work, you are likely to be protected by state **Workers' Compensation** laws. These laws provide a fixed schedule of benefits for medical care and certain disability income benefits, as well as rehabilitation expense reimbursements.

Medical coverage may also be provided in certain homeowner's and automobile insurance policies, and by Medicare for citizens 65 years of age and older.

Physical disability can mean more than lost income. Resultant expenses can include rehabilitation, recuperation, medicine and drugs, nursing, and miscellaneous medical costs. Intangible costs can also result: the psychological depression the disabled breadwinner may suffer, the extra demands imposed on other members of the family, and concern over what prospects the future holds.

Certain ongoing programs may already be protecting your income: the sick pay plan at your place of employment, Workers' Compensation, Social Security, unemployment insurance, waiver of premium provisions in your life and health insurance policies, credit health insurance included in loan agreements, and other personal assets. Disability income insurance is also available in a vast variety of sizes and shapes. You may obtain an individual policy directly through a company, or you may obtain a policy on a group basis, such as through a professional association, a union, or a trade group.

One of the most important factors in shaping a disability income plan is the waiting period, the amount of time you have to be disabled before the insurance begins to pay benefits. It's possible to obtain a policy that will begin payment of benefits on the very first day of disability due to accident. Or you might obtain a policy with a waiting period of 15, 30, 60, 90 days or longer. Once the disability payment begins, the policy may have limits on how long or how much you will be paid.

Some disability insurance policies agree to pay you a flat fixed amount in the event you are totally disabled. Should you be partially disabled, the company will pay you a portion, usually half, of the full disability benefit. The definition of total disability can be very important. In some cases, you must be totally unable to perform any kind of work in order to receive total disability benefits.

Benefits that you receive from a disability income program are not subject to income taxes, so it's not necessary for you to try to obtain a monthly benefit that's equal to your actual income.

Learning Objectives

When you complete this lesson, you should be able to:

- □ Describe the three major parts of a typical health insurance protection program.
- □ Explain how major medical insurance works.
- □ List the advantages of a health maintenance organization.
- □ Discuss the purpose of Workers' Compensation.
- □ Cite at least three sources of income and disability insurance available to workers.

Reading Assignment

Read Chapter 19 of the text, "Life, Health, and Income Insurance," pages 499–523.

Key Words and Phrases

- □ **Disability income insurance**—Insurance that provides some income to a worker who becomes unable to work because of injury or health problems.
- □ **Health maintenance organization (HMO)**—A prepaid medical care facility.
- □ **Hospital insurance**—A form of insurance policy that reimburses the insured for costs of being hospitalized, including room, board, and other specified services.
- □ **Major medical insurance**—A form of health insurance designed to protect the insured against heavy, even catastrophic, health care expenses.
- □ **Medicare**—A health insurance program administered by the Social Security Administration for the protection of citizens 65 years old and over.
- □ **Nursing home insurance**—A new insurance phenomenon that pays a daily benefit to the insured for nursing home care. Most policies have a 20-day waiting period and stipulate that hospitalization must have preceded nursing home admission for benefits to become payable.
- □ **Physician insurance**—A form of health insurance that pays doctor bills within stated limits.
- □ **Surgical insurance**—A form of health insurance that reimburses the insured for surgical and related expenses.
- □ **Unemployment insurance**—A state-administered insurance program, paid for by employers, that provides financial benefits to employees who are laid off.
- □ **Workers' Compensation**—A state-administered health and disability program, paid for by employers, that provides certain benefits to workers who suffer job-related injuries or illnesses.

Self-Test

1. Hospital insurance is needed to cover operating room expenses.
a. true
b. false

2. One of the primary advantages of a major medical health insurance plan is that the insured is usually covered for the full cost of a physician's or surgeon's fee.
a. true
b. false

3. Consumers who want to save money should discontinue their regular health insurance program once they become eligible for Medicare and Medicaid.
a. true
b. false

4. Automobile medical insurance is a good alternative to the three basic types of health insurance.
a. true
b. false

5. If one chooses a higher deductible, the cost of health insurance can be reduced.
   a. true
   b. false
6. If you are hospitalized, which of the following types of health insurance is needed to cover the cost of room and board?
   a. hospital insurance
   b. major medical insurance
   c. physician insurance
   d. surgical insurance
7. Your physician insurance company has just reimbursed your doctor for $400 of the $700 total bill. What type of insurance would you need to reimburse you for all or part of the remaining $300?
   a. disability insurance
   b. major medical insurance
   c. surgical insurance
   d. Workers's Compensation
8. A deductible is usually associated with
   a. hospital insurance.
   b. major medical insurance
   c. physician insurance.
   d. surgical insurance.
9. Which of the following clauses in a health insurance policy states that you do not have to make premium payments during periods of disability?
   a. double indemnity clause
   b. extended premium clause
   c. loss of income clause
   d. waiver of premium clause
10. The health insurance plan that requires the insured to pay a fixed fee each month to a medical facility, whether medical services are required or not, is
    a. hospital insurance
    b. health maintenance organization.
    c. Medicare.
    d. Worker's compensation.
11. This state insurance plan protects workers for expenses related to injuries or illness resulting from their job.
    a. disability insurance
    b. sick pay plan
    c. unemployment insurance
    d. Workers' Compensation

Using What You've Learned

Title: The Terminal Patient

Purpose: One of the major areas of misunderstanding concerning health insurance coverage involves the terminally ill patient, especially cancer victims. Most health insurance plans pay the hospital costs only for a person who is being cured. Since many hospitalized cancer patients are being treated for "comfort" and not for cure, the health insurance company may deny coverage. This project enables you to investigate this situation and develop a plan of action that would apply if you or a family member became the victim of a lengthy terminal illness.

Description:

Visit your local doctor and health insurance agent to obtain information on insurance coverage for a terminally ill person. Find out the doctor's experience in dealing with insurance coverage for these patients. Second, contact a health insurance agent and find out his or her company's position on providing medical coverage for terminally ill individuals.

Task:

Based on your findings, answer the following questions.

Summarize the doctor's remarks

Summarize the insurance agent's remarks

Describe your plan of action for coping with a lengthy terminal illness.

CHAPTER

22

Financial Planning for Later Years

Overview

There comes a time for everyone when a plateau that might be referred to as "financial maturity" is reached. This time generally coincides with those years when children have grown and moved out on their own. As you reach financial maturity, your needs and attitudes toward a great many important financial matters are in a state of change. These matters include housing, investing, insurance, use of leisure time, and the ultimate direction of your working career. Many of the financial decisions made during your twenties and thirties can have a profound bearing on your ability to fulfill goals during the mature years.

Housing requirements are often drastically altered with the onset of financial maturity. Personal feelings can stand between you and the money that could help provide added security and comfort in the years ahead. It's a choice between retaining the old family homestead with its comforts and memories and exchanging it for another dwelling that may be more practical and economical.

Most homeowners in their forties and fifties have substantial equity in their homes. Additionally, the value of the property has probably increased considerably. One of the main financial advantages of home ownership, the deductibility of mortgage interest and real estate taxes, may be of far less value to homeowners in the later years, particularly after retirement. And the cost of maintaining a home may be burdensome.

If the house is sold, a house or apartment could be rented, or another house purchased. Even if the monthly expenses are higher, the profit from the sale of the old house could be invested and the income applied toward housing expenses, leaving the nest egg intact.

If the house is not sold, refinancing an existing mortgage might be considered if current interest rates are equal to, or less than, the interest on the existing mortgage. Otherwise, refinancing would be of little benefit.

Investing

Investment attitudes and tactics are likely to undergo a considerable change as you reach the plateau of financial maturity. Until that point, generating capital to meet the expenses of housing, educating children, and other family needs are the primary concern. With those needs substantially accomplished, you turn to the preservation of capital. While you're young you can afford to make mistakes and still recoup. As the years go by, the specter of financial loss via investments is more fearsome. You may not have the time or the ability to recover.

Financial maturity brings accompanying changes in your insurance program. The life insurance program designed to protect a family in the event of the premature death of a breadwinner may no longer be appropriate. Because age renders you more susceptible to the risks of injury and illness, the ability to cope with these circumstances becomes increasingly important.

Retirement

The older person faces career decisions. How long do you want to continue working? If you intend to continue, what kind of employment might be available to someone with your skills, desires, experiences, and needs? If mandatory retirement is not in your future, when will you voluntarily begin to taper off and how quickly? Will you want to take some new direction in your career; try something you've always wanted to do?

How much will you have to live on when your active working career tapers off or ceases altogether? Inflation can be an ominous specter, particularly if retirement income is fixed and the ability to work has diminished or disappeared. Beyond the natural reduction in spending that accompanies diminished family responsibilities, some conscious steps can be taken to lessen expenses. The effects of inflation may also be blunted by Social Security and pension payments with escalation clauses that are tied to rising prices.

There are two primary sources of sustenance to be considered in detail: income and principal. Income is money received from all sources such as Social Security, pensions, investments, and work. Principal is accumulated money working for you that may be dipped into for living purposes as the need arises. The most prudent approach is to attempt to live on the income and keep the principal in reserve.

In September of 1974, Congress passed the Employee Retirement Income Security Act of 1974, more commonly known as the Pension Reform Law, or ERISA. The purpose of the law was to correct abuses in the administration of pension funds that resulted in pensioners being deprived of monies that were due them. The Pension Reform Law attempts to correct vesting, funding, folding, reporting, and management abuses.

The Tax Reform Act of 1986, in conjunction with Social Security regulations, will have an impact on the time at which retirees will be entitled to full benefits from their pension plans. The 1986 Tax Reform Act states that an employee must be at least 65 years of age before he or she can receive 100 percent of the pension benefits. Further, the law sets forth a gradual increase in the minimum retirement age, again in line with the Social Security formula.

There is no one—no company, no government, no union—who can take as good care of your future as you can. Pension and profit-sharing plans may hold the promise of future security. Social Security, as structured in the late 1980s, might not enable participants in their forties and younger to get out of Social Security what they put in. Unless changes are made, it might be foolhardy for people in the younger generations even to think of relying on Social Security as more than a token portion of their overall retirement income. And Congress has begun to tax Social Security benefits—a philosophy that could increase as years go by.

Do-it-yourself retirement planning is enhanced by a variety of plans that offer attractive advantages to those who participate. These plans are the Individual Retirement Account (IRA), the Simplified Employee Pension (SEP), and the 401 (k) plans for employed individuals, and the Keogh plan for self-employed individuals.

There are two major income tax advantages to IRA plans. The first advantage is that the earnings in your IRA plan are tax-deferred: You don't pay income taxes on your IRA earnings until such time as you cash in your plan and spend the money for your own purposes. The second major advantage is that the amount you invest in an IRA each year is tax-deductible if you are not covered by a retirement or profit-sharing plan at work. If you are covered by such a plan at work, your right to claim the annual deduction is determined by how much you and your spouse earn. The law states that if you withdraw your IRA money before your reach the age of 59-½, you must pay a penalty to the government and whatever income taxes are due on that withdrawn money. The law also requires that you begin withdrawing money from your IRA plan when you reach the age of 70-½.

If the company you work for offers a 401 (k) plan, a certain portion of your wages will be placed in an investment program offered by the employer. Those wages will not be taxable until you later withdraw the funds. The earnings will also be tax-deferred. A 401 (k) plan can be very advantageous, particularly if the employer is contributing on your behalf over and above what you are putting in.

A relatively uncommon form of do-it-yourself retirement program is the Simplified Employee Pension (SEP). This concept operates similarly to an IRA. The employer can make contributions to the IRAs that the workers maintain on their own. And the workers can also make their own contributions.

Keogh plans are available to self-employed individuals. The maximum amount of an annual Keogh investment is $30,000 or 25 percent of income from work, whichever is less. Keogh investments are tax-deductible to the participant, and earnings are tax-deferred. Withdrawals from Keogh plans are similar to those from IRAs: There's a penalty for withdrawals made before age 59-½, and a withdrawal program must begin by age 70-½. Keogh plans do have further complexities involving the types of plans that can be set up and how much can be contributed to each one. It's advisable for individuals contemplating a Keogh plan to get professional assistance from their own tax adviser or from the institution in which they're opening the plan.

IRAs, Keoghs, and SEPs can be set up relatively simply at banks, savings institutions, stock brokerage firms, mutual fund companies, and insurance companies.

You should begin as far in advance as possible to estimate your retirement benefits and the impact taxes will have. The potential sources of gross income include Social Security, pension, profit-sharing, and IRAs. But it's the net amount, after taxes, that's important.

Learning Objectives

When you complete this lesson, you should be able to:

- □ Devise a strategy to help retired people living on a fixed income cope with inflation.
- □ Explain how life insurance can be used as a source of funds during retirement years.
- □ Discuss the housing dilemma that faces retired individuals.
- □ List at least five income sources, other than Social Security, that might be used to supplement retirement income.
- □ Outline the effects of the 1974 Pension Reform Law on the rights of workers and retirees.
- □ Explain how vesting protects the worker.

Reading Assignment

Read Chapter 20 of the text, "Financial Planning for the Later Years," pages 524–554.

Key Works and Phrases

- □ **401 (k) plan**—A do-it-yourself retirement investment plan, available only to employees of companies that offer the plan.

- **Funding**—The placing of money in a pension plan by an employer. Proper funding requires that enough money be placed in the fund to meet future promises to pay benefits to covered employees.
- **Individual Retirement Account (IRA)**—A do-it-yourself retirement investment plan with attractive tax benefits, available to all workers.
- **IRA rollover**—Reinvestment of a lump-sum payout from a pension or profit-sharing plan (within 60 days of receipt) into an account designated as your IRA rollover account.
- **Keogh plan—A do-it-yourself retirement investment plan with attractive tax benefits, available to self-employed persons.**
- **Pension Benefit Guarantee Corporation (PBGC)**—A federal insurance program that guarantees retirees a continuation of at least a portion of their promised pension benefits if the company or the pension plan fails.
- **Pension Reform Law of 1974** (Employee Retirement Income Security Act, ERISA)—A federal law that protects the rights of employees with respect to pension and profit-sharing plans.
- **Simplified Employee Pension (SEP)**—An uncommon do-it-yourself retirement investment plan for small companies that operates similarly to an IRA.
- **Vesting**—A concept that pertains to one's pension benefits becoming irrevocably due; vesting occurs according to a preset schedule.

Self-Test

1. One of the advantages of a fixed income portfolio is that it allows retired people to predict with reasonable certainty how much money they will have available at any given future time.
   a. true
   b. false
2. Inflation is one of the biggest problems facing retired people.
   a. true
   b. false
3. Because Social Security payments fluctuate with the Consumer Price Index, this form of retirement income can be classified as fixed income.
   a. true
   b. false
4. If you are a full-time employee for more than 10 years, your employer must set up a pension plan for you in accordance with the requirements specified in the Pension Reform Law of 1974, even if the company has not yet offered a pension plan to any of its other employees.
   a. true
   b. false
5. Funding refers to putting enough money into a pension fund to meet future promised benefits.
   a. true
   b. false
6. The current federal law states that individuals who are entitled to benefits under a pension or profit-sharing plan may be given the choice of receiving those benefits in one lump sum or in a program of monthly payments.
   a. true
   b. false

7. The wise consumer should begin to plan financially for the retirement years
   a. at age 60.
   b. after age 65.
   c. as soon as possible.
   d. around age 50.
8. Regarding planning for financial retirement, which of the following statements is most accurate?
   a. The typical American can depend on Social Security benefits to provide financial security upon retirement.
   b. Private pension plans offer the best source of retirement income.
   c. Individuals can best plan their own financial retirement providing they take early steps to do so.
   d. People who live in the United States should rely on the government to support them in their retirement years.
9. The main purpose of the Pension Reform Law of 1974 is
   a. to correct abuses that occurred in the administration of pension funds.
   b. to create a pension system that will gradually replace the Social Security System.
   c. to require all employers to offer a pension plan to their employees.
   d. to restrict the pension rights of self-employed individuals.
10. Which of the following refers to the point at which your pension benefits are guaranteed as a result of the time you have spent on the job?
    a. funding
    b. income investing
    c. Individual Retirement Account
    d. vesting
11. Which of the following is not true concerning Individual Retirement Account rollover?
    a. Funds cannot be withdrawn from the account before the age of 59½ without penalty.
    b. Funds must be initially withdrawn from the account by age 70½.
    c. Funds invested earn interest on a tax-deferred basis.
    d. After age 59½, funds invested earn interest that is subject to federal income taxes.
12. The federal agency that guarantees retirees a continuation of at least a portion of their pension benefits should the company providing such benefits go out of business is called
    a. funding
    b. Individual Retirement Account
    c. Pension Benefit Guarantee Corporation.
    d. vesting.

Using What You've Learned

Title: The Retired Person

Purpose: By interviewing a retired individual, you will develop an appreciation of the social and financial implications associated with the retirement years. The information obtained will be useful in planning for retirement.

Description: Interview two or three retired individuals or couples.

Task: Based on the information obtained in your interview, answer the following questions.

What did they fear most about retirement?

What social problems do they encounter?

What are their sources of income?

How do they rate the Social Security benefits they receive?

What pension do they receive?

Are they encountering any financial difficulties?

What is their worst fear now?

If they had the opportunity to plan their retirement years differently, what would they do?

___

___

___

What advice can they offer you?

___

___

___

Based on the text material and the information received from the interview, briefly outline a list of considerations to keep in mind when planning your retirement.

___

___

___

___

___

___

___

___

___

CHAPTER

23

Estate Planning: The Tools You'll Use

Overview

One of the most important, and most overlooked, aspects of personal financial concern is estate planning. While living, your **estate** is all that you own, less all your debts. After death, your estate becomes a legal entity in its own right.

Estate planning is the development of a program that ensures that your last wishes are carried out. There are many devices to establish such a program. The most common is the will. Other devices include life insurance, gifts, trusts, and simply spending it all, leaving nothing behind.

If you do not choose to establish a plan for the disbursement of your estate, the laws of the state of residency at the time of death will determine its distribution. Each state has its own laws, known as **laws of intestacy.** All state laws are somewhat similar, yet different.

Although the right of the individual to determine the distribution of his or her accumulated wealth after death is deeply rooted in our legal tradition, certain limitations have been imposed over the years. For example, the federal and state governments are entitled to a portion of the estate.

There are several tools that can be used to minimize this tax bite and pass wealth to heirs and other generations.

- **Wills.** A will is the most common device used in the formation of an estate plan.
- **Trusts.** A trust is a "strings-attached" way of passing money or property to another party. The trust agreement itself can stipulate just how much the beneficiary will get at what time and under what circumstances.
- **Gifts.** Making gifts of money or property is another form of estate planning.
- **Insurance.** For a great many families, life insurance is the predominant way of passing wealth from one generation to the next.
- **Joint ownership.** Putting property in joint names, such as husband and wife, is a simple way to ensure that the surviving spouse will receive everything after the death of the other spouse.
- **Spending it all.** The spending is easy. The difficulty lies in knowing how to coordinate final spending and final expenses.

In a sense, a **will** is a form of contract: it is a legally binding document that sets forth certain rights and responsibilities of the parties, and it cannot be changed without the consent of at least the person who drew up the will. The major clauses of a will set forth primary responsibilities and rights:

- **Introductory clause.** This generally is the opening clause of a will and should clearly and unmistakably state, "This is my last will and testament," or "My will is as follows." It is essential that this clause establish that you are creating the will and that the document is, in fact, your will.
- **Revocation.** If you are creating a new will, to replace one previously made, your should clearly revoke the entire prior will be stating so clearly in the new will.
- **Debts, final expenses.** Before your survivors can receive their share of your estate, the remaining debts, funeral expenses, and taxes must be paid. Commonly, testators include a clause in their wills instructing executors to make these payments.
- **Legacies, bequests.** These clauses determine which survivor gets how much. Broadly speaking, there are four ways in which property can pass to the survivors: through joint ownership with right of survivorship; through a specific bequest; through a general bequest; or through the residuary. A specific bequest refers to a particular item or security. General legacies are those payable out of the general assets of the estate. Everything that's left after distribution by joint ownership and specific and general legacies is called the residual.
- **Appointment clause.** In this clause, the testator appoints the person or institution who will be the executor of the estate.
- **Execution, witnesses.** The final clauses of a will are called the testimonium clause and the attestation clause. In the **testimonium clause,** a testator states that the document is a last true will and testament, as of the date of execution. The **attestation clause** relates to confirmation by the witnesses that they have witnessed the signing of the will in the presence of the testator and of one another.

A will that is prepared in the handwriting of the testator is called a **holographic will.** Some states permit the probate of holographic wills under certain circumstances, but such wills are definitely not a substitute for a will prepared under proper legal guidelines.

In more extreme cases, a will may be spoken by the dying individual to another party or parties. Such an oral will is referred to as a **noncupative will.** It's allowed only by some states, and then only under strictly defined conditions.

When the testator dies, the attorney for the estate, generally acting in conjunction with the executor, will request that the appropriate court commence the probate proceedings. All potential heirs will have been notified and will be given the opportunity to accept or challenge the will as written. A would-be heir who wishes to challenge an otherwise valid will has to do so at his or her own expense, which can be considerable.

Your will and overall estate plan should be reviewed at least every three years. Some circumstances might dictate the need to amend a will or any other portion of an estate plan. A will can be legally changed in one of two ways: it can be totally revoked by a new will, in which case the new one should expressly state that the former will is totally revoked; or minor changes can be effected by means of a brief document called a **codicil.** A will cannot be legally amended by crossing out or adding words, by removing or adding pages, or by making erasures.

Where at all possible, proper legal assistance should be sought in creating a will. A store-bought will, with blanks to be filled in, or a will prepared under the instructions of a "do-it-yourself" guidebook is false economy. Saving the legal fees involved in creating an estate plan could result in a far more costly and aggravating situation. A do-it-yourself will can be either invalidated or contested, creating bitterness among the survivors. Such a will can also subject the estate to unnecessary taxation.

Learning Objectives

When you complete this lesson, you should be able to:

- □ Define a will, and state its major purpose.
- □ Differentiate between estate taxes and inheritance taxes.
- □ State why the executor/executrix is an important part of estate planning.
- □ Discuss the purpose of a probate proceeding.
- □ List and briefly explain the basic clauses of a will.
- □ Compare a regular will to an uncommon will.
- □ Define a trust, and state its main purpose.
- □ Discuss the importance of using an attorney to prepare a will.

Reading Assignment

Read Chapter 21 of the text, "Estate Planning" pages 555–570.

Key Terms and Phrases

- □ **Administrator/Administratrix**—A court-appointed person responsible for handling the estate of a person who died without a will.
- □ **Attestation clause**—A clause in a will in which the witnesses to the will confirm that they have performed their duties in accordance with the law.
- □ **Beneficiary**—One who receives an inheritance from the estate of a decedent.
- □ **Bequest**—The specific property or money given to a beneficiary from the estate of a decedent.
- □ **Codicil**—A document that, when properly executed, amends a will.
- □ **Decedent**—One who has died.
- □ **Estate**—The legal entity that comes into being upon the death of a person; for example, upon John's death, his estate comes into being. Also refers to the net worth of the decedent; for example, John's estate is worth $100,000.
- □ **Executor/Executrix**—The person or institution designated by a testator to carry out the settlement of the testator's estate.
- □ **Holographic will**—A will prepared in the handwriting of the testator; not always valid.
- □ **Intestacy**—The status of one who dies without a will. In such a case, the law of the state in which the decedent resided determines how the estate is to be distributed.
- □ **Life estate**—A form of bequest wherein the recipient has the use of the property in question only for the remainder of his or her life, after which it passes to someone previously named by the original testator.
- □ **Noncupative will**—A will that is spoken by the testator to another party; not usually valid.
- □ **Probate**—A court proceeding in which the validity of a will is proved.
- □ **Testator/Testatrix**—A person who makes a will.
- □ **Testimonium clause**—A clause in a will in which the testator states that he or she is signing the document as his or her last will and testament.
- □ **Trust**—An arrangement whereby one person or institution (the trustee) has custody of someone else's (the trustor's) money or property for ultimate distribution to a named thirty party (the beneficiary). An **inter vivos trust** is one

that comes into being while the trustor is alive. A **testamentary trust** is one that comes into being upon the death of the trustor.

- □ **Trustee**—The individual or institution designated to administer a trust.
- □ **Will**—A document that, when properly drawn and executed, assures the protection of the state court over the distribution of the testator's estate in accordance with his or her wishes as expressed in the document.

Self-Test

1. Estates, being legal entities in their own right, may be required to pay estate taxes.
a. true
b. false

2. The most obvious purpose of an estate plan is to document who will get the money and property of the deceased.
a. true
b. false

3. If a person dies without having made a will, the person is said to have died with an uncommon will.
a. true
b. false

4. A codicil is a will in which minor changes have been made by crossing out or adding words, removing or adding pages, or by making erasures.
a. true
b. false

5. Once a will has been drawn and executed, the original copy should be kept by the attorney.
a. true
b. false

6. A person who makes a will is referred to as the
a. administrator.
b. beneficiary.
c. executor/executrix.
d. testator/testatrix.

7. Which of the following refers to the legal court proceeding in which the validity of a will is established?
a. bequest
b. codicil
c. probate
d. testimonium

8. The purpose of the attestation clause in a will is to
a. confirm that the witnesses have performed their duties in accordance with the law.
b. name the beneficiary.
c. name the administrator.
d. cancel all prior wills.

9. Which of the following estate planning approaches will help to reduce estate taxes?
a. gifts made prior to death
b. utilizing life insurance proceeds to distribute funds
c. using an uncommon will
d. naming more than one beneficiary

10. The estate of a person who dies without a will is subjected to state laws called
   a. gift tax laws.
   b. inheritance tax laws.
   c. intestacy laws.
   d. state income tax laws.

11. If you want to leave part of your estate to your son but do not want him to have the money until 10 years after your death, you could use which of the following devices to make the arrangements?
   a. joint account
   b. probate
   c. trust
   d. holographic will

Using What You've Learned

Title: Preparing Your Will

Purpose: You will develop an appreciation of the importance of the contents of a will by actually preparing a draft copy of your own will.

Description: If you have not already done so, prepare a draft of your own will, using the format outlined in Table 23-1. Review the textbook sections entitled "The Language of Estate Planning" and "The Will," pages 559–567, to guide you in preparing your own will.

CHAPTER 24

Estate Planning: Achieving Your Objectives

Overview

To think that an estate plan is something that pertains only to one's death is a mistake. The creation of a sound estate plan can and should be an integral part of your goal-setting endeavors, discussed early in this telecourse.

There are four main objectives to keep in mind when creating or amending any estate plan:

- establishing the proper liquidity and distribution of assets
- establishing a program of sound management of assets
- providing for the assured continuation of a family's life-style in the event of death, disability, or retirement
- minimizing taxation

Distribution of assets and liquidity of those assets go hand in hand. **Distribution** refers to "who gets what." **Liquidity** refers to the ability to put cash on the table as quickly as possible and with as little expense as possible. The most important reasons for liquidity are to provide for the immediate needs of survivors—spouse, children, and other survivors—and to pay any estate taxes when they are due.

Proper management of assets in an estate is a factor all too often overlooked. Management can be accomplished in a number of ways. Assets can flow through a trust arrangement whereby income is paid to the survivors, who can have the right to tap the principal for specific purposes as and if the need arises. Insurance policies can also be arranged so that the money is paid out over an extended period rather than in one lump sum. Extended withdrawal plans can also be set up with annuities, mutual funds, and pension and profit-sharing plans.

Sound financial planning requires continued attention to potential estate tax liability. With proper advance planning, the costly bite of estate taxes can be minimized. Three kinds of taxes that can arise when a person dies are:

- **Estate taxes.** When a person dies, his or her estate becomes a legal entity. If the estate is large enough, the federal government will levy a tax on the value of the estate.
- **Inheritance taxes.** Some states levy an inheritance tax. This is a tax that is paid by those who receive inheritances.
- **Income taxes.** Many months, if not years, can elapse before an estate is distributed to all the heirs. During that time, assets of the estate may be invested and receive income. In such cases, the income received is subject to income taxes.

Extensive changes in estate and gift tax laws went into effect at the start of 1982. One of the most important had to do with marital deductions. The **marital deduction** consists of that portion of an estate that is left, in proper legal fashion, to one's surviving spouse. For deaths occurring in 1982 or after, there is generally no limit to the amount of marital deduction that can pass from one spouse to the other. This applies whether the transfer of wealth occurs before or after death.

Effective in 1988, an individual can make gifts to as many persons as he or she wishes, but if those gifts exceed $10,000 per recipient per year, the amount in excess of $10,000 is subject to taxation at the same rates as the estate tax rates. An estate that might otherwise be subject to taxation can be reduced considerably by making gifts over a period of years.

In doing the estate planning necessary to minimize taxes, consider the estate of the surviving spouse. If a surviving spouse remarries, he or she may not wish the second spouse to share in the inherited estate. As is often the case, the surviving spouse might prefer to have the inherited estate pass on to his or her own children. But the effect of "cutting out" the second spouse is to eliminate the availability of the marital deduction, and this, in turn, can increase the potential estate tax.

If a surviving spouse does not remarry, there would be no marital deduction available at all. The estate would be subject to maximum taxation unless the surviving spouse had taken other steps to minimize the tax burden.

In planning your estate, you will need the assistance of a number of professionals, including financial advisers, accountants, insurance experts, and lawyers.

Learning Objectives

When you complete this lesson, you should be able to:

- □ List and briefly discuss the four major objectives to consider when creating or amending an estate plan.
- □ Outline an approach that can be used to manage the assets of an estate effectively.
- □ List and describe the three kinds of taxes that may be levied on a decedent's estate.
- □ Illustrate with figures how the marital deduction can be used to decrease federal estate taxes.
- □ Describe three federal estate tax avoidance devices that can be used in estate planning.

Reading Assignment

Read Chapter 21 of the text, "Estate Planning," pages 570–585.

Key Terms and Phrases

- □ **Credit against taxes**—For all deaths occurring in 1987 and after, an estate with taxable transfers of less than $600,000 is not subject to federal estate taxes.

- □ **Estate taxes**—A federal or state tax on the estate of a decedent.
- □ **Gross estate**—Everything that an individual owns or that is owed to the individual.
- □ **Heir**—One who receives an interest in the estate of a decedent.
- □ **Inheritance tax**—A state tax on individuals who receive inheritances.
- □ **Marital deduction**—The portion of one's estate that is left, in proper legal fashion, to the surviving spouse. The marital deduction amount reduces the taxable portion of the estate.
- □ **Taxable transfer**—With respect to federal estate and gift taxes, the amount on which the tax is figured after having taken into account all proper deductions.

Self-Test

1. The best way to implement an estate plan is with the aid of a capable attorney.
a. true
b. false

2. As with all other elements of estate planning, the matter of the management of assets must be reviewed from time to time and amended as needed.
a. true
b. false

3. In order to avoid conflicts between members of the family, the prudent estate planner should not communicate with them about what each expects from the state.
a. true
b. false

4. The costly bite of estate taxes can be legally minimized if one does not report all of the decedent's assets to the government.
a. true
b. false

5. No matter how well you plan your estate, all estates must pay a minimum federal estate tax of 18 percent of the total estate.
a. true
b. false

6. In general, inheritance taxes are state-imposed taxes.
a. true
b. false

7. An estate that might otherwise be subject to taxation can be reduced considerably by providing beneficiaries with gifts—small portions of the estate—over a period of years prior to death.
a. true
b. false

8. In creating an estate plan, you should first
a. read several textbooks on the subject.
b. visit with a qualified attorney to discuss estate planning objectives.
c. consult the federal government.
d. get advice from friends on how they created their estate plan.

9. Which of the following refers to the ability to put cash in the hands of those the deceased wanted to receive cash as quickly and with as little expense as possible after his or her death?
a. distribution of assets

b. estate tax reduction
c. liquidity of assets
d. management of assets

10. Of the following, which will generally consume the largest portion of an estate?
a. federal estate taxes
b. federal income taxes
c. federal inheritance taxes
d. federal excise taxes

11. This tax is paid by the heirs of an estate after the estate has been distributed:
a. state distribution taxes
b. state estate taxes
c. state inheritance taxes
d. state transfer taxes

12. The portion of an estate that is left, in proper legal fashion, to one's surviving spouse is called
a. joint deduction.
b. marital deduction.
c. spouse allowance.
d. taxable transfer.

Using What You've Learned

Title: Why Pay Estate Taxes?

Purpose: Given a hypothetical situation, this project will provide you with the opportunity to take a list of assets held by an individual and develop a distribution plan that will preserve as much of the estate as possible for the decedent's family.

Description: Bruno Spencer is 46 years old; his wife Mariann is 38. They have three children, age 13, 15, and 19. Bruno has just been informed that he has a terminal illness and is not expected to live for more than a year or two. He has discussed the situation with his family and prepared a list of his current assets, which he would like to distribute to his family upon his death.

- **House.** The house is jointly held with his wife. It is fully paid for and has a current value of $250,000.
- **Common stock.** Held in his name and valued at $150,000.
- **U.S. Savings Bonds.** Held in his name, with his wife as beneficiary; valued at $25,000.
- **Corporate bonds.** Held in his name; valued at $30,000.
- **Stamp and coin collections.** Valued at $35,000.
- **Cash on hand.** $25,000.
- **Life insurance policy.** His wife is the owner and beneficiary of the policy. Coverage is $200,000.

Bruno would like to satisfy all his family members when his estate is settled, but he is especially concerned about his wife. He also wants to provide the funds necessary to assure a college education for his three children. He is also concerned about minimizing federal estate taxes and state inheritance taxes.

Task: Prepare a list of suggestions to help Bruno plan for the settlement of his estate.

PART SEVEN

INCOME TAXES: HOW TO BITE BACK

CHAPTER

25

How Income Taxes Work

Overview

Federal income tax has become an ever-present influence in the management of personal financial matters. Investment decisions, recordkeeping disciplines, retirement planning, and day-to-day budgetary matters are all affected, for better or for worse, by income tax implications.

In 1986, Congress passed a sweeping Tax Reform Act. It necessitated many new and complicated forms, calculations, phase-ins, and phase-outs that will last until 1991 and beyond. The Tax Reform Act of 1986 was the fourth major overhaul of income tax laws in a 10-year period. It certainly will not be the last. And as the laws change, so, perhaps, must your own financial plans if you want to take advantage of what the law allows or escape any disadvantages the law may impose.

With hundreds, perhaps even thousands, of dollars at stake in your own tax return, it's essential to be aware of all the possible ways to keep your taxes at the legal minimum. To an extent, a professional tax specialist can help you gain this awareness. But the specialist spends only a few hours a year with you. He or she may not think to ask, and you may not remember, all the transactions you conducted during the year that could have tax consequences. Your awareness of the tax laws will help you to be a better recordkeeper and a better manager of your financial affairs.

Of all the income you receive in a year, only some of it is taxable. There are many ways that the total amount of your income can be reduced to find the taxable portion. And once that taxable portion is determined, there are ways to minimize the taxes you owe on that income. Following, in brief, are the steps you'll take:

1. Accurately list all your taxable income.
2. Reduce that total by the proper legal methods—adjustments, deductions, and exemptions
3. Figure the lowest possible tax by choosing the right filing status and claiming all proper credits.

The first important choice you have to make in preparing your return is your **filing status.** There are five possible choices. Many taxpayers can qualify for more than one status, but choosing the wrong one can result in higher taxes.

Married taxpayers can choose to file separate returns, or they can file together on a joint return. With few exceptions, it will be to their benefit to file a joint return.

Unmarried taxpayers may be able to choose from the other three filing statuses: single, head of household, and qualifying widow(er). Of these choices, the single status will pay the highest tax, followed by the head of household and the qualifying widow(er).

For every **exemption** you can legally claim, you are allowed to reduce your taxable income. You are entitled to claim one exemption for yourself and, if you are married, you can claim one exemption for your spouse. In addition, you may claim exemptions for every person who is your legal dependent.

All legally taxable income must be declared. As noted earlier, care should be taken not to report any income that is not taxable. Items of taxable income include: wages, salaries, and tips; interest income; dividend income; and alimony received. If you receive certain other types of income, you will be required to complete additional detailed schedules: business income and loss, Schedule C; capital gains and losses, Schedule D; and pensions, annuities, rents, royalties, and partnerships, Schedule E. Other types of taxable income include fees for services you perform; property you receive through barter; gambling winnings; prizes and awards received as a result of drawings, television programs, and the like; and part or all of any unemployment insurance benefits you receive.

You may receive nontaxable money from various sources. These items should not be reported on the income part of your 1040 form. Some of the more common types of nontaxable income include some types of interest income, accident and health insurance proceeds, life insurance proceeds, gifts and inheritances, Social Security benefits, scholarships, fellowships, and grants.

The first main category of expenses that can be used to reduce your total income are **adjustments.** You may be required to fill out separate schedules or forms with respect to the claiming of some of these adjustments.

- □ **Payments to an IRA or Keogh plan.** You may be able to claim an adjustment to your income for the investments you make in these retirement plans in a given year.
- □ **Alimony paid.** As noted earlier, alimony received is taxable income. On the other hand, alimony paid is an adjustment that can be used to reduce your total income.

Certain types of expenses are identified as **deductible** from your income. These expenses include medical expenses, charitable contributions, taxes, interest, casualty or theft losses, and other expenses related to your ability to generate income.

Whether you have actually incurred such expenses, the law allows you to claim a certain fixed amount of such deductions. This is known as the **standard deduction.** If you have, in fact, spent more on deductible items than the standard deduction allows, you are entitled to claim all those expenses as deductions. But you must itemize each and every one of them, and you must have evidence that you did, in fact, incur such expenses. If you do itemize your deductions, you will be required to complete Schedule A of the 1040 form.

Other miscellaneous expenses can be deducted only to the extent that they exceed 2 percent of your adjusted gross income for the year.

Now you've reached the point where the tax can be calculated using the tax rate tables provided by the Internal Revenue Service.

Once you've computed your tentative tax, you can reduce it further if you are entitled to any of the credits allowable in the current year. Every dollar's worth of credit reduces your tax by one dollar.

Learning Objectives

When you complete this lesson, you should be able to:

- □ Define and explain the difference between earned income and unearned income.
- □ Define the term "exemption," and list the steps required for someone to qualify as an exemption.

- □ Recognize why the selection of the filing status is important to the taxpayer.
- □ Differentiate between a standard deduction and an itemized deduction; between the purposes of Schedules A and B.
- □ Explain the various methods that can be used to reduce one's taxable income.
- □ Indicate how income averaging can be used by the taxpayer.
- □ Indicate when an amended tax return should be used.

Reading Assignment

Read Chapter 22 of the text, "Income Taxes" pages 587–609.

Key Terms and Phrases

- □ **Adjustments to income**—In calculating one's income taxes, a main category of expenses that can be used to reduce the amount of income that is subject to taxation.
- □ **Amended tax return**—A tax return that may be filed after the original return was filed to correct errors in the original return.
- □ **Deductions**—Regarding income taxes, a category of expenses that is subtracted from adjusted gross income to lower the amount of income subject to taxation. Taxpayers may claim itemized deductions or standard deductions.
- □ **Exemptions**—With regard to income taxes, the number of persons dependent on the taxpayer, including the taxpayer. For each proper exemption the taxpayer is allowed to reduce the income subject to taxes by a fixed amount.
- □ **Filing status**—One of five categories chosen by taxpayers as a part of completing their returns; the choice of category, which is broadly based on taxpayer's marital status, affects the amount of tax payable.
- □ **Forms 1040, 1040A, and 1040EZ**—The basic forms used to file one's federal income taxes. Taxpayers who wish to claim certain adjustments, credits, and itemized deductions use the 1040 (long form). Taxpayers who do not wish to claim these items use the 1040A (short form) or the 1040EZ.
- □ **Itemized deductions**—A specific listing of all allowable expenses that can be used to reduce the amount of income subject to taxation.
- □ **Nontaxable income**—Money received by a taxpayer that is not subject to income taxes, such as inheritances and life insurance proceeds.
- □ **Schedules A and B**—Federal income tax forms, used in conjunction with the 1040 form for declaring itemized deductions (A), income from interest and dividends (B).
- □ **Standard deduction**—For taxpayers who choose not to itemize their deductions, this is a fixed amount that can be used to reduce the amount of income subject to taxation. This deduction may be taken whether or not the taxpayer actually incurred such expenses. Also known as zero bracket amount.
- □ **Tax credit**—An amount that may be deducted from one's computed federal income tax. Every dollar's worth of credit reduces your tax by one dollar. Common credits include the credit for child care expenses and the residential energy credit.
- □ **Tax rate schedule**—With respect to federal income taxes, the format from which certain taxpayers calculate their taxes due.
- □ **Taxable income**—In calculating taxes payable, the income on which the tax is figured after all proper deductions, exemptions, and adjustments have been taken into account.

Self-Test

1. Without exception, every American who earns money during the year is legally required to file an income tax return for that year.
   a. true
   b. false
2. Unearned income is generally income from investments as opposed to earned income, which is income from work.
   a. true
   b. false
3. To qualify as an itemized deduction, contributions to qualified charitable organizations must be in the form of cash.
   a. true
   b. false
4. If you make certain mistakes in calculating your federal income taxes, which lead to your paying more taxes than necessary, the IRS
   a. is obligated to correct your error.
   b. will automatically refund the excess taxes to you.
   c. will gladly accept the extra taxes you paid.
   d. will fine you.
5. Which of the following individuals is not likely to have a tax obligation?
   a. a student who earns $8,000 by working part-time
   b. a retired person, age 65, who received $6,500 in Social Security benefits
   c. a stock investor who earns a total of $45,000
   d. a married couple with four children and an income of $56,000, filing a joint return
6. If a person wants to itemize deductions, he or she must use which of the following forms?
   a. Form 1040A
   b. Form 1040EZ
   c. Form 1040 and Schedule A
   d. Form 1040
7. Which of the following is classified as nontaxable income?
   a. child support money
   b. alimony
   c. interest earned on corporate bonds
   d. Series HH U.S. Savings Bonds
8. Which of the following statements applies to interest earned from an Individual Retirement Account (IRA)?
   a. the total interest is tax-exempt
   b. the interest is not taxable in the year in which it was earned, but will be taxable in some future year
   c. the interest is fully taxable in the year it was earned
   d. the interest is considered taxable only if posted to a passbook account
9. Which of the following is an example of an adjustment to income?
   a. gambling losses
   b. commuting to and from work
   c. Social Security taxes
   d. payments to an IRA plan
10. This federal income tax procedure permits you to deduct certain expenses on your tax return, whether or not the expenses have actually been incurred:

a. income averaging
b. itemized deductions
c. joint return
d.. standard deduction

11. Which of the following is not classified as an itemized deduction?
a. credit card interest
b. medical bills
c. property insurance premiums
d. union dues

12. Once you have computed your tentative tax, this factor allows you to reduce your tax obligations further:
a. adjustments to income
b. deductions
c. exemptions
d. tax credit

Using What You've Learned

Title: Completing the Tax Form

Purpose: Personal and financial information will be provided so that you can gain experience with the long and short federal tax forms. You will need a copy of this year's forms 1040A, 1040, and Schedule A, and tax tables. You may obtain copies by visiting or calling your local IRS Office.

Description: Patricia Fitz is an administrative assistant who works for a New York publishing company. She is single and is entitled to one exemption. In January, she received her Form W-2 from her employer, stating that her wages for the year were $17,560, and that federal taxes withheld were $3,821. Patricia does not itemize deductions and wants to report her income to the federal government on a 1040A form.

John and Mary Jordon both work. They have two children: Keith and Kevin. John works at a local bank and received a total of $25,224 in wages last year; his employer withheld $3,271 in federal income taxes. Mary is a secretary, and her employer reported wages of $15,500 from which $2,011 federal income tax was withheld.

In addition to their wages, the Jordons earned $155 in interest on their joint savings account, and $340 in dividends. John also won $595 at the racetrack. Both John and Mary want to contribute to the Presidential Election Campaign Fund.

The Jordons are going to claim the following deductible expenses for the year:

Medical	
Insurance	$400
Drugs and medicines	300
Doctors and dentists (not covered by insurance)	350
Eyeglasses	300
Taxes	
State and local income	$1,018
Real estate	1,200

Interest	
Mortgage	$4,800
Credit cards	240
First National Bank	50
Contributions	
Church	$550
United Fund	600
Miscellaneous	
Union Dues	$80

One winter day, John lost control of his car on an icy street and had a collision, resulting in damages to his auto that cost $650 to repair. He carried no collision insurance.

Task: Using the information given, complete a 1040A form for Patricia Fitz and a 1040 form and Schedules A and W for the Jordons.

CHAPTER

26

Tax-Saving Strategies

Overview

If you don't claim all the exemptions, adjustments, deductions, and credits to which you are entitled, the Internal Revenue Service won't do it for you. Throughout the year it's your job to make certain that you keep track of all those items and incorporate them into your tax return. Similarly, there are other tax-cutting strategies you can use.

To the extent feasible, take advantage of opportunities to earn tax-exempt or tax-deferred income. You can earn **tax-exempt income** by investing in municipal bonds or in mutual funds that specialize in municipal bonds. **Tax-deferred investment income** is available through insurance companies, commonly in conjunction with stock brokerage firms. Some of your income from work may also be invested on a tax-deferred basis. This is particularly so with pension and profit-sharing plans.

Individual Retirement Accounts (IRA) and **Keogh plans** can be ideal ways to defer taxes income from work and investments. A relatively new device that allows you to earn tax-deferred income is the 401 (k) plan, if your employer offers such a plan. U.S. Savings Bonds series EE also offer the opportunity to earn tax-deferred income.

Of the more than 100 million tax returns filed annually, over 80 percent get a refund from the government. The reason these taxpayers get a refund check is that they have had more of their pay withheld by the employer than was really necessary to meet their annual obligation. The government holds those excess payments and then returns them to the taxpayer in the form of a refund check once the taxpayer has filed his return for the year.

An employer is required to withhold from workers' pay enough to meet each worker's obligations for the year. The employer estimates the amount that must be withheld each pay period based on the information the employee provides on a W-4 form.

The more allowances an employee claims, the less is withheld from his or her pay. The best strategy is to see to it that your W-4 reflects the correct number of allowances to which you are entitled.

As each calendar year draws to a close, you should try to estimate your tax liability for the current year and compare it to what you anticipate for the following year. The reason for doing this is to try to determine whether it would make sense to shift income or deductions from one year to the next in order to cut your tax obligation. The overall strategy behind such moves is to claim deductions in years in which you'd be most highly taxed and to receive income in years when you'd be taxed less.

Shifting income or deductions need span only a few weeks—from late December into early January. If much more time than that is involved, the shifting may be counterproductive, since the loss of use of your money for more than a few weeks might offset the value of the shifted income or deductions. Examples of shifting income include year-end bonuses that could be declared or paid in early January instead of late December; payment for fees or services; sales that result in capital gains.

Regulations set forth by the Tax Reform Act of 1986 make it possible for a family with children to cut their income taxes somewhat by making gifts of income-producing assets to children. The tax saving is based on the general assumption that children do not earn as much income as their parents and are thus taxed in lower brackets or are not taxed at all.

With rare exceptions, the Tax Reform Act of 1986 effectively slammed the door on the tax breaks that had been available through shelter schemes. However, despite the continuing efforts of Congress to close all tax loopholes and keep them closed, new loopholes are constantly being created. And as new loopholes are created, sales pitches are created to lure your dollars. Then, within a few years, congressional clamor will close those loopholes. And so the cycle goes.

At any given time, there may be tax advantages available in a variety of investments and speculative schemes. It's up to the prudent investor and sensible taxpayer to examine any such opportunities thoroughly, to exercise caution with respect to the enthusiasm of the salesperson, and to proceed with the knowledge that today's tax break could be eliminated tomorrow. If you do claim deductions or credits arising out of what the IRS would consider a tax-shelter scheme, you increase your chances of being audited by the IRS.

The law allows you an opportunity to get an extention on your filing date, and it also allows you to correct a return already filed if the need arises. Regulations in recent years have allowed taxpayers an automatic four-month **extension** for the filing of their individual returns. In order to obtain the automatic extension, you must file a Form 4868 with the IRS center in your area by the regular due date (April 15). The extension of the time to file your return is **not** an extension of the time to pay taxes.

Once you've filed your return for any given year, you can **amend** it later if you determine that you owe the government or that they owe you a refund because you didn't claim exemptions, adjustments, deductions, or credits to which you were entitled. The form to use to amend your return is 1040X. The law allows you ample time to file an amended return: three years from the date you filed your original return, or two years from the time you paid your tax, whichever is later.

All returns are checked clerically to determine that the arithmetic is correct and to make certain that the returns and any checks attached thereto have been properly completed and signed. A further screening determines whether there are errors in the return with respect to deductions, exemptions, and the like.

In recent years, the IRS has been auditing about 2 percent of all individual returns filed. About 70 percent of the returns chosen for audit are selected by the **discriminate income function,** or DIF. Returns are examined by computers, and specific elements of the return are scored. These elements include your total income, adjusted gross income, deductions, adjustments, and credits. Based on past statistical evidence, agents can determine which returns—by virtue of the scoring—have the greatest potential for recovering additional taxes through an audit. About 8 percent of all returns chosen for audit are selected via the **Taxpayer Compliance Measurement Program (TCMP).** This is a random selection by the IRS computers and/or agents and is considered to be a much more comprehensive audit. Aside from these two procedures, the following are generally regarded as red flags that will prompt an IRS audit:

- an individual with income over $50,000, particularly if there are tax-sheltered deductions involved

- □ excessive deductions for travel and entertainment expenses
- □ deductions claimed for the expense of maintaining an office in your home
- □ losses arising out of what the IRS determines to be a hobby, even though you determine it to be an ongoing business

If you are audited, and you and the IRS agent agree on the findings at your initial meeting, you will be asked to sign a form stipulating the content of the agreement. Shortly thereafter, you will receive a written report plus a bill for the additional taxes you owe, including any interest or penalties that have been agreed on.

If you are unable to settle the matter in the IRS office audit, you should immediately ask for a written copy of your legal rights. You can also ask for an immediate meeting with a supervisor, in the hope that such a meeting might result in a more favorable compromise.

If you don't reach an agreement with the supervisor, the agent will send you a report explaining the additional tax liability. You then have the right to request a conference at the district level to see if the matter can be resolved. If a settlement still isn't reached at the conference level, you'll receive a Notice of Deficiency, commonly referred to as a 90-day letter. In this letter, the government notifies you that you will be assessed the additional tax owed 90 days from the date the letter is mailed. If you still believe your case is valid, you can:

- □ file a petition with the tax court
- □ pay the tax and then file a refund claim for that amount
- □ if the amount is less than $5,000, proceed in the relatively new Small Claims Division of the tax court

There is nothing that can insulate you better from the rigors of a tax audit than an accurate return accompanied by all the proper documentation for all claims made. Having all the documentation is the difference between an audit's being a minor inconvenience and a costly source of stress.

Learning Objectives

When you complete this lesson, you should be able to:

- □ Define and give an example of the following tax-reducing strategies: tax-exempt and tax-deferred income, income splitting, and tax shelters.
- □ Indicate the relationship between the W-4 form and take-home pay.
- □ Describe the procedure necessary to file a late tax return.
- □ Explain the purpose of an amended tax return and recognize when it should be used.
- □ Suggest at least five strategies that could be used by the taxpayer to avoid the possibility of an audit.
- □ List at least five steps that will help you answer an audit inquiry.

Reading Assignment

Read Chapter 22 of the text, "Income Taxes" pages 609–624.

Key Terms and Phrases

- □ **Audit**—The procedure in which the Internal Revenue Service examines in detail one's income tax return.
- □ **Discriminate income function (DIF)**—A computerized procedure used by the IRS to select tax returns for audit. The computer compares various elements of a given return (income, deductions, etc.) and further compares those ratios to average levels for such claims.
- □ **Filing extension**—Available to taxpayers who file the proper form; an added time to file their tax return.
- □ **Income shifting**—The procedure whereby a high-bracket taxpayer transfers income-producing assets to low-bracket taxpayers, such as his or her children, so that the income will be taxed at a lower rate.
- □ **Tax shelter**—A type of investment, usually speculative in nature, that enables a taxpayer to reduce his or her income taxes.
- □ **Taxpayer Compliance Measure Program (TCMP)**—A random selection by the Internal Revenue Service of tax returns to be audited.
- □ **W-4 Form**—A federal tax form in which a worker claims a number of allowances, which in turn determine the amount of tax withheld from the worker's pay.

Self-Test

1. The interest earned from municipal bonds is an example of a tax-exempt source of income.
a. true
b. false

2. The chief advantage of an Individual Retirement Account is that the interest earned on that account is never subject to federal income taxes.
a. true
b. false

3. The strategy underlying income splitting is to shift the tax burden from an individual in a high tax bracket to one in a lower tax bracket.
a. true
b. false

4. Tax laws allow a taxpayer to file a tax return after the April 15 deadline if the proper form is completed.
a. true
b. false

5. In general, only 2 to 5 percent of all individual tax returns are checked for arithmetic and clerical errors.
a. true
b. false

6. Which of the following is an example of a tax-deferred investment?
a. municipal bonds
b. dividend income
c. Individual Retirement Account interest
d. tax-shelter interest expense

7. Most taxpayers receive a refund check each year because
a. they make errors on their 1040 form.

b. they had more of their pay withheld by their employer than was necessary to meet their tax obligation.
c. the IRS changed the tax brackets, resulting in lower taxes.
d. the IRS fails to audit most returns that claim a refund.

8. Having your year-end bonus paid in Janaury instead of December is an example of
a. amending the return.
b. income splitting.
c. shifting income.
d. a tax shelter.

9. If you discover an error on a previously filed tax return, you should
a. write the IRS office and explain why the return was wrong.
b. file an amended tax return Form 1040X.
c. ignore the error if reporting it would mean more taxes.
d. report the error on the next tax return.

10. Your chances of being audited by the IRS are
a. about 50/50.
b. almost a certainty.
c. nil if you do not itemize deductions.
d. under 5 percent.

11. Which of the following items refers to the IRS's random selection of tax returns to be audited?
a. amended return
b. discriminate income function
c. related pickups
d. Taxpayer Compliance Measurement Program

Using What You've Learned

Title: The Not Too Cool Taxpayer

Purpose: This project will provide you with an opportunity to develop a strategy for coping with an IRS audit, from the point of view of a taxpayer who appears to have made some mistakes.

Description: A.J. Mangoldie has just received notification from the IRS that his tax return of last year is being audited. The IRS has asked him to offer a response to each of the items listed in the following table. They would like him to submit any additional information, including written evidence and receipts.

Task: In the space provided in the table, make some suggestions to help A.J. answer each inquiry.

IRS Question	Suggestions
A $500 contribution to his church	

IRS Question	Suggestions
Union dues of $420 paid	
An itemized deduction for contribution of $500 to the A. J. Mangoldie Animal Humane Society for the care of his pet dog, Murph	
A deduction of $8,500 for the purchase of a home minicomputer to assist him in preparing his income tax records and returns	
Failure to report state lottery winnings of $2,500	
Exemptions claimed for three children although he filed as a single. On the previous year's return, he had no exemptions for children listed.	
An itemized deduction of $756 claimed for the repair of his automobile	
An itemized deduction of $3,000 claimed for the loss of a gold wedding ring	

Based on the eight items listed, the IRS has calculated that he owes an additional $6,500 in federal income taxes. In addition to the suggestions that relate to the items listed previously, what other advice and suggestions can you offer A.J.?

____

____

____

____

____

____

Answer Key

1 The Economy

1. b	**5.** b	**9** c
2. b	**6.** d	**10.** c
3. a	**7.** a	
4. a	**8.** b	

2 Work, Income, and Your Career

1. a	**5.** b	**9.** b
2. a	**6.** b	**10.** a
3. b	**7.** d	**11.** a
4. b	**8.** d	**12.** c

3 Creating a Workable Plan

1. a	**5.** a	**9.** c
2. b	**6.** b	**10.** d
3. b	**7.** d	**11.** c
4. a	**8.** a	**12.** a

4 The Smart Shopper

1. b	**5.** a	**9.** b
2. a	**6.** b	**10.** a
3. a	**7.** b	**11.** a
4. b	**8.** a	

5 Frauds and Swindles

1. b	**5.** a	**9.** d
2. a	**6.** a	**10.** d
3. b	**7.** c	**11.** c
4. a	**8.** c	**12.** b

6 Transportation

1. a
2. a
3. a
4. a
5. b
6. a
7. d
8. b
9. d
10. c
11. b
12. a

7 Leisure and Recreation

1. b
2. a
3. a
4. a
5. a
6. b
7. b
8. b
9. a
10. d
11. c

8 Buying a Home

1. a
2. b
3. a
4. a
5. a
6. a
7. a
8. d
9. b
10. b
11. d
12. c

9 Financing a Home

1. b
2. a
3. b
4. b
5. a
6. a
7. a
8. d
9. b
10. c
11. a
12. a

10 Housing Costs and Regulations

1. b
2. a
3. a
4. a
5. a
6. a
7. b
8. a
9. c
10. b
11. c
12. a

11 Renting

1. a
2. a
3. b
4. a
5. b
6. b
7. a
8. d
9. b
10. a
11. a
12. c

12 Selling Your Home

1. b	**5.** a	**9.** a
2. a	**6.** b	**10.** d
3. a	**7.** c	**11.** d
4. b	**8.** a	**12.** d

13 Financial Institutions

1. a	**5.** b	**9.** a
2. a	**6.** b	**10.** d
3. b	**7.** c	**11.** d
4. b	**8.** d	**12.** c

14 Credit and Borrowing

1. a	**5.** b	**9.** b
2. b	**6.** a	**10.** c
3. a	**7.** b	**11.** d
4. b	**8.** b	**12.** d

15 Making Your Money Grow

1. b	**5.** a	**9.** c
2. b	**6.** b	**10.** b
3. a	**7.** a	**11.** b
4. a	**8.** d	

16 The Money Market

1. a	**5.** b	**9.** c
2. b	**6.** a	**10.** d
3. a	**7.** b	**11.** b
4. b	**8.** a	**12.** a

17 The Stock Market

1. b	**5.** b	**9.** c
2. b	**6.** b	**10.** c
3. b	**7.** a	**11.** d
4. a	**8.** c	**12.** b

18 Real Estate Investments

1. b	5. a	9. d
2. a	6. b	10. c
3. a	7. a	11. b
4. b	8. d	

19 Other Investment Opportunities

1. a	5. b	9. d
2. a	6. a	
3. a	7. d	
4. b	8 b	

20 Life Insurance

1. a	5. a	9. a
2. b	6. a	10. d
3. a	7. c	11. b
4. a	8. b	12. d

21 Health and Income Insurance

1. b	5. b	9. d
2. b	6. a	10. b
3. b	7. b	11. d
4. b	8. b	

22 Financial Planning for Later Years

1. a	5. a	9. a
2. a	6. a	10. d
3. b	7. c	11. d
4. b	8. c	12. c

23 Estate Planning: The Tools You'll Use

1. a	5. a	9. a
2. a	6. d	10. c
3. b	7. c	11. c
4. b	8. a	

24 Estate Planning: Achieving Your Objectives

1. a	5. b	9. c
2. a	6. a	10. a
3. b	7. a	11. b
4. b	8. b	12. b

25 How Income Taxes Work

1. b	5. b	9. d
2. a	6. c	10. d
3. b	7. a	11. c
4. c	8. b	12. d

26 Tax-Saving Strategies

1. a	5. b	9. b
2. b	6. c	10. d
3. a	7. b	11. d
4. a	8. c	